Academic Honors in Princeton University

ACADEMIC HONORS

IN

PRINCETON UNIVERSITY

IN

PRINCETON UNIVERSITY

1748–1902

COMPILED AND EDITED

BY

JOHN ROGERS WILLIAMS

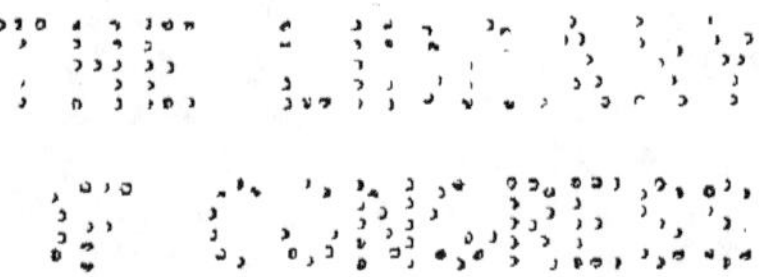

PRINCETON UNIVERSITY

OFFICE OF THE SECRETARY

1902

PREFACE

This volume contains a list of the Latin and English
Salutatorians, Valedictorians, Honormen, Junior Orators,
Lynde Debaters, Prizemen, Fellows, First Group Men, and
University Debaters, from the first Commencement in 1748
until the present day.   It is unfortunately incomplete for the
years 1750 –'53, 1755 –'59, 1763 –'64, 1776 –'77, and in minor
detail, a careful search through the files of nearly all the
current newspapers, from which source the honormen for the
first seventy-five years have been obtained, has failed to
supply the omissions.   In 1757 and in 1777, however, the
public exercises of Commencement were omitted, and it is
believed no honors were assigned   The absence of official
source-material, notably the Minutes of the Faculty, for the
eighteenth century and a period of some twenty years in
the nineteenth, has made the task of collation one of the
greatest difficulty, which will account for the fragmentary
nature of the record during the early years of College history.

From 1748 until 1835, the honors have been compiled
from the published accounts of the Commencements which
appeared in the various newspapers of the day, supple-
mented by the Minutes of the Faculty where extant, by
biography and history, and the manuscript records of the
University   From 1835 until 1902, they are taken from the
Minutes of the Faculty and the official lists of honormen
printed in the yearly catalogues.

Unless otherwise specifically stated in the notes, the arrangement of the honormen is in the order of their standing, where the Minutes of the Faculty are available, they have been strictly followed in this particular Since the adoption of the system of honor groups by the University in 1886, the names under each group are arranged in alphabetical order.

The work of compiling this volume was undertaken at the suggestion of Mr. M Taylor Pyne, '77, to whom the editor is further indebted for valuable advice and assistance. He has also been courteously assisted by the librarians of the New York Public Library, the State Library of New Jersey, and the Pennsylvania Historical Society, while at work among their collections, and by many other persons ; which indebtedness is most gratefully acknowledged.

J. R. W.

Princeton, N. J., September 15, 1902

CONTENTS

INTRODUCTION

INTRODUCTION

———

Commencement Honors

The following statement of the origin and relative importance of the various honors and prizes, will be found of use in connection with the text.

The custom of awarding honorary orations, to be delivered at the annual Commencement as a token of good scholarship, had its origin with the founding of the College. Of these orations the Latin Salutatory is the oldest, dating back to the first Commencement in 1748   It was ordinarily awarded to the student attaining the highest individual rank in scholarship, and still maintains its distinctive quality as the highest honor at the disposal of the Faculty.

The Valedictory was probably first awarded as a graduation honor in 1760   Prior to this it was delivered by a candidate for the degree of Master of Arts   It was usually awarded to the best orator of the class, without regard to academic standing, of late years, however, scholarship is also taken into account with the qualifications of the student as a Valedictorian

In 1786 a Second Latin Salutatory oration was awarded, doubtless to the next highest in standing; this was changed the year following to a Greek Salutatory, which in 1788 became the English Salutatory, for more than an hundred years the second honor. This oration was discontinued in 1897

Other honorary orations were added from year to year, the Mathematical in 1792, the Belles Lettres in 1793, the Theological and Moral Science in 1804, and others Orations denoting excellence in the various arts and sciences were regularly awarded during the last century, but have since been discontinued.

PRIZES

Witherspoon in his "Address to the Inhabitants of Jamaica," published in Philadelphia in 1772, gives the following account of the competitions for prizes which were then held the day before Commencement

"On the day preceding the Commencement last year there was (and it will be continued yearly hereafter) a public exhibition and voluntary contention for prizes, open for every member of College These were first, second, and third prizes, on each of the following subjects. 1 Reading the English language with propriety and grace, and being able to answer all questions on its Orthography and Grammar. 2 Reading the Latin and Greek languages in the same manner with particular attention to true quantity. 3 Speaking Latin. 4. Latin versions. 5 Pronouncing English orations The preference was determined by ballot, and all present permitted to vote, who were graduates of this or any other College."

The first of these competitions was held in 1771 Upon this occasion Aaron Burr received the English prize, Henry Brockholst Livingston the Latin, Henry Lee the prize for "Turning English into Latin," and William Bradford that for public speaking. These exercises were probably discontinued about the year 1800, with the exception of an isolated contest in 1815. The prizes awarded in 1815, according to the Minutes of the Faculty, were books, and the names of the successful candidates were publicly mentioned on Commencement day. As the only account of these contests exists in the newspapers of the period, a complete record is impossible

Dickinson Prize

In 1782, Governor John Dickinson, of Delaware, presented to the Trustees his note for £100, suggesting that the interest be applied in procuring a gold or silver medal to be awarded for the best dissertation on one of several named subjects   But one dissertation was presented in 1783, and the President was directed to republish the subject the year following without award   For several years this medal was awarded, but the students took little interest in it and the competitions were abandoned   In 1871, upon complaint being made to the Trustees by some of the descendants of Governor Dickinson that the fund had been diverted from its original purpose, a committee was appointed to investigate the matter   This committee later reported that the Board had received from Governor Dickinson the sum of £100 currency, and that the interest, save for a few years, had never been applied in the manner designated by the donor. They recommended that one thousand dollars be appropriated to reestablish the Dickinson Prize Fund, and that the interest be used for the purpose originally intended. This report was adopted, and the first award under the new endowment was made at the Commencement of 1872.

Minto Medal

It is recorded in the Minutes of the Trustees that, in 1789, Dr Walter Minto, then Professor of Mathematics and Natural Philosophy, gave a medal of the value of five pounds to be competed for at that Commencement   There is no mention of any later award

Junior Orations and Junior Orator Medals

The custom of holding contests in oratory, usually on the day preceding the annual Commencement, had its origin early in College history. The first contest of this kind, open to all undergraduates, was held in 1771   These exercises continued regularly for several years and became a feature of the Commencement. About the year 1802 a material change took place in the method of choosing the competing orators , eight were selected, four from each Literary Society, so that the exercises became in reality contests between the American Whig and the Cliosophic Societies. Later the competitors were chosen entirely from the Junior class, and were known as "Junior Orators." For many years these contests rivalled in popularity the graduating exercises of the Senior class, becoming in no small degree a feature of the academic year, and bitter was the warfare waged by the two Halls in pursuit of honors. Mention of the distribution of these honors, prior to 1865 when medals were first awarded to the successful contestants, has been omitted, as no authentic data for such a record exists

On December 20, 1864, a committee of Trustees was appointed to decide upon the matter of Junior Orator prizes; this committee later reported favorably (June 28, 1865), and the following resolution was adopted   "That the Faculty be empowered to procure four gold medals, costing fifteen dollars each, and have them suitably inscribed ; and to present them to the young gentlemen to whom prizes were awarded by the Committee on Junior Orators " The value of the medals has since been increased to twenty dollars.

The choice of representatives was originally with the Societies themselves, but the disorders consequent upon these elections, amounting in some cases to "riots" and "acts of violence," according to the Trustee Minutes, forced the Board to change the manner of their appointment The first measure was to authorize the Faculty (1859) to make the appointments of Junior Orators independent of any action taken by the student members of the Societies. In 1864 it was decided that the selection of speakers should be made by the Faculty, after a fair trial of the merits of the different candidates At present the orators are chosen by committees appointed by the two Societies from their own members in the Faculty.

Leonard W Jerome Prizes

In 1866 Mr. Leonard W. Jerome, of New York, donated five thousand dollars to establish a fund, the interest from which was to be expended in the purchase of two medals or other testimonials to be awarded to members of the graduating class It is not clear from the Minutes upon what basis the awards were to be made. Popularity apparently was the chief requisite, as the selection was to be determined by ballot, each member of the Senior class having the right to vote for the person who, in his opinion, was best entitled to the distinction, and the medals were to be awarded to the two, one from each Literary Society, who received the greatest number of votes. The students, however, refused to accept the prizes, and the money was returned several years later at the request of donor, without any award having been made.

Class of 1859 Prize in English Literature

In 1869, the Class of 1859, through its representatives, Alfred Hosea Kellogg, Henry Everett Russell, and Samuel Richards Colwell, conveyed to the Trustees two thousand dollars in trust, for the establishment of a prize foundation in English Literature, open to members of the Senior class. The first award was made in 1870.

George Potts Bible Prizes

Mrs Sarah A. Brown, of Princeton, in 1866 gave one thousand dollars to found a prize in Biblical study, the interest of which was to be expended in the purchase of two copies of Matthew Henry's Commentary, to be presented annually to the two best Biblical scholars of the Senior class Awards have been made annually since 1869

Experimental Science Prize

In 1870 a prize of one hundred dollars was offered by the Faculty to the member of the Senior class who should pass the highest examination in Experimental Science It was not again proposed , the only award was made in 1870

Maclean Prize

The Maclean Prize, of the annual value of one hundred dollars, was first awarded in 1872 It was founded by the will of Henry A Stinnecke of the class of 1861 The following extract from the will, probated in 1866, is of interest:

" I further direct that a sum, the annual income of which shall amount to one hundred dollars, shall be applied by the said Trustees to the founding of the Maclean Prize, which prize shall be given to that one of the Orators chosen by the Literary Societies from the Junior Class. who shall on the night before Commencement, or at such other time as the Junior Orations shall be held, pronounce the best English Oration

" The Commmittee that shall award said prize shall consist of the Professor of Rhetoric ' ex officio,' and two graduates of the College not members of the Faculty, the latter to be appointed by the Trustees

" I found said prize as a Memorial of my esteem and regard for Dr John Maclean, President of the College, and of my hearty appreciation of the kindness shown to my classmates and to me during our College course '

Stinnecke Scholarship

The Stinnecke Scholarship was also established by the will of Henry A. Stinnecke, '61   It is awarded to the member of the Sophomore class "who shall pass the best examination at the opening of the session in September, in the Odes of Horace, the Eclogues of Vergil, and the Latin Grammar and Prosody, as well as the Anabasis or Cyropædia of Xenophon and the Greek Grammar "   It is of the annual value of five hundred dollars, and is tenable during the undergraduate course.   The first award was in 1873

Class of 1861 Prize

The interest of twelve hundred dollars, given by the Class of 1861, is annually awarded to the member of the Sophomore class passing the best examination at the end of the year in Mathematics.   It was established in 1872.

Junior First Honor Prize

In 1870, and thereafter until 1876, Mrs John R. Thomson gave two hundred dollars to the best scholar of the Junior class In 1875 this prize was endowed by a bequest from Miss Maria Stinnecke, the annual interest of which amounted to two hundred dollars. It was known for several years as the "Miss Stinnecke Scholarship," and was awarded to the Junior first honorman until 1882, when upon receipt of the Wood legacy it was combined with the H. A Stinnecke endowment

In 1880 a legacy was received from George Bacon Wood, M D , the annual income of which amounts to one hundred and fifty dollars. This has been awarded to the Junior first honorman since 1883

Science and Religion Prize

In 1872, Furman Sheppard, of the class of 1845, offered a medal valued at one hundred dollars, or its equivalent in money, to be given to the member of the Senior class who should pass the highest examination in the Harmony of Science and Revealed Religion This prize was offered annually until 1887, when it was discontinued.

Anonymous Prizes

In 1873, also in 1874 and in 1875, several prizes were offered by "a graduate of the College," as follows

A prize of fifty dollars to the member of the Senior class offering the best essay on a given subject in Political Economy

A prize of fifty dollars to the member of the Senior or Junior class offering the best essay on a given subject in Mental Philosophy

A prize of fifty dollars to the member of the Junior class writing the three best essays in English Literature during Junior year

A prize of fifty dollars to the member of the Junior class writing the best essay in French Literature upon a given subject

A prize of one hundred dollars to the member of the Sophomore class passing the best examination in Greek and Latin upon certain named subjects

A prize of one hundred dollars to the member of the Sophomore class standing highest at the Biennial Examination

A prize of one hundred dollars to the member of the Freshman class passing the highest examination in the subjects required for entrance

Freshman First Honor Prize

A prize of two hundred dollars to be given to the member of the Freshman class attaining the highest average in scholarship, was established in 1873 by a deed of gift from John S Kennedy, Esq , of New York. This prize was awarded with the provision that it should not be given to the student taking the Stinnecke Scholarship. It was discontinued in 1900.

Lynde Debate Prizes

Mr Charles R. Lynde in 1876 donated five thousand dollars to establish a prize fund in debate. Three prizes, representing the income of this sum, are awarded by a committee appointed by the Faculty, to the successful competitors in a debate held during Commencement The competitors in this debate, six in number, of the Senior class, are chosen from the American Whig and the Cliosophic Societies by a committee of their own members in the Faculty The first prize was originally of the value of one hundred and thirty dollars , the second, one hundred and twenty dollars, and the third, one hundred dollars, but the decrease in the rate of interest has lessened their value They are at present worth one hundred, eighty-three, and sixty-six dollars, respectively   The first contest was held during the Commencement of 1876.

The Stinnecke Prizes

In 1877 three prizes, of the value of seventy, forty, and thirty dollars, respectively, from the income of the Stinnecke legacy, were awarded to the three members of the Sophomore class having the highest standing during Sophomore year   The awards were discontinued in 1880.

The Baird Prizes

Charles O Baird, Esq , in 1882 offered the following prizes, open to members of the Senior class .

The Baird Prize of one hundred dollars to the best writer and speaker, a prize for Oratory of fifty dollars to the next best speaker and writer, and a prize of fifty dollars for the best poem, and of fifty dollars for the best written disputation delivered at the public oratorical exercises of the Senior class

Through the liberality of the same donor, the Baird Prize fund was established the year following by a gift of six thousand dollars, and the number of prizes offered was increased   At present they are .

The Baird Prize of one hundred dollars, to the best speaker of those who have ranked among the first six writers, in any two of the three departments of English Literature, Rhetoric, and Oratory

A prize for oratory, of fifty dollars, to the best speaker, exclusive of the Baird Prizemen, of those who in the same departments have ranked among the first twelve writers

A prize for delivery, of thirty dollars, to the best speaker, exclusive of the above

A prize for poetry of fifty dollars

Two prizes of forty and thirty dollars respectively for the best and the second best written disputations

The Lyman H. Atwater Prize in Political Science

In 1883 the Class of 1883 established a prize fund of one thousand dollars, as a memorial of the Rev Lyman H Atwater, D D , LL.D , Professor of Political Science, who died during that year   The annual interest from this sum is awarded to the member of the Senior class who is adjudged to have passed the best examination and written the best essay upon a given subject in the department of Political and Social Science   This prize was first awarded in 1885

The Alexander Guthrie McCosh Prize

Founded in 1885 by a gift of one thousand dollars from President James McCosh to establish a prize in memory of his son Alexander Guthrie McCosh   The endowment was increased by a further gift of five hundred dollars from President McCosh in 1889   The interest is annually awarded to the member of the Senior class passing the best examination and writing the best essay upon a given subject in Philosophy.   The first award was in 1886.

The Francis Biddle Prize

Founded in 1887 by a gift of five hundred dollars from Henry W Biddle, Esq , in memory of Francis Biddle of the class of 1875   The interest is yearly awarded to the member of the Sophomore class, not below fourth group, who in the judgment of a committee appointed by the Faculty, shall write the best English essay   It was first awarded in 1888

Frederick Barnard White Prize in Architecture

Established in 1887 by a yearly gift of fifty dollars from Mrs Norman White, in memory of her son, Frederick Barnard White, of the class of 1883 In 1890, Mrs White gave one thousand dollars to the University to permanently endow this prize It is open to members of the Junior and Senior classes, and is awarded for the best essay upon some given subject in Architecture

The Class of 1876 Prize for Debate in Political Economy

Established in 1887 by a gift of one thousand dollars, which has since been increased to two thousand, from the Class of 1876. This prize, at present the income from two thousand dollars, is awarded to the successful contestant in a debate on a subject of current interest in American politics, to be held on Washington's Birthday. The competitors, four in number, one from each class, are chosen by a vote of their respective classes.

Theodore Cuyler Prize in Economics

Established in 1889 by a gift of one thousand dollars from Cornelius C. Cuyler, of the class of 1879. In 1896 Mr. Cuyler added four thousand dollars to his former gift Competition for this prize is open to members of the Senior class ; it is awarded for the best examination and thesis on some stated subject in Political Economy It was first offered in 1890

The Thomas B Wanamaker English Prize

Founded in 1889 by a gift of bonds valued at one thousand dollars from Thomas Brown Wanamaker, Esq., of the class of 1883. This prize, of the value of fifty dollars, is awarded to the member of the Junior class passing the best examination in English Philology, who shall also write the best thesis on some topic therein.　The first award was in 1890.

George W Childs Preliminary Entrance Examination Prizes

Established in 1889 by a yearly gift of fifty dollars from George W. Childs, Esq., and awarded to the student from Philadelphia or vicinity, passing the best preliminary entrance examination into the Academic Department.　In 1893 and afterward, prizes were awarded to both Academic and Scientific students, under the same conditions　The awards were first made in 1890 and were discontinued in 1896.

Class of 1870 English Prizes

In 1890 the Class of 1870 gave the sum of two thousand five hundred dollars to establish a prize fund in English, designated and applied as follows

Class of 1870 Junior English Prizes　Of the yearly interest of one thousand five hundred dollars, one-half will be given to the best Old English scholar, and one-half to the best English Literature scholar of the Junior Academic class

Class of 1870 Sophomore English Prize　The yearly interest of one thousand dollars will be given to the member of the Sophomore Academic class who, at the close of Sophomore year, shall pass the best examination in the English studies of the year

The first award was made in 1891.

The C O Joline Prize in American Political History

Two hundred and fifty dollars, the gift of Adrian H. Joline, Esq., class of 1870, was received in 1890 to found "The C. O. Joline Prize in American Political History." An annual prize of the value of fifty dollars was offered for five years to the member of the Senior class passing the best examination in American Political History (1789–1820), who should also write the best thesis on an assigned topic connected with that period In 1896 the prize was renewed, under different conditions, by a second gift of two hundred and fifty dollars. It was then specified .

The sum of one hundred and fifty dollars, payable in annual installments of fifty dollars, will be awarded at intervals of not less than three years to that graduate of the University, pursuing the study of American History as a specialty, who shall have presented before graduation the best thesis on some topic assigned by the Professor of History, and connected with the political history of the United States between the years 1787 and 1820, and who shall annually, for two years thereafter, present as evidence of his work a satisfactory essay of not less than five thousand words on a kindred topic suggested by himself

This prize was first offered in 1891 , it has not been awarded since 1896.

New York Herald Prize

Founded by James Gordon Bennett, Esq., in 1893 by a gift of one thousand dollars. The prize is awarded to the member of the Senior class, or to the special student of satisfactory standing, who shall have taken the prescribed course in Political Science and English Literature, and who shall have prepared the best essay in English prose upon some subject of current interest in the domestic or foreign policy of the United States. The first award was in 1894.

The M C. H Junior German Prizes

Founded in 1898 by the late Professor Willard Humphreys in memory of his mother, Mary Cunningham Humphreys. These prizes, of the value of twenty-five and fifteen dollars respectively, were paid annually by Professor Humphreys during his life, and since his death, September 26, 1902, the principal sum of one thousand dollars, by a provision in his will, has been given to the University. The first awards were made in 1899. The prizes are given to the members of the Junior class (Academic) who, having taken the regular German course for at least two years, shall, at the close of the second term, pass the best examination on the work of the term, and on the life of the author whose works have been the principal subjects of the year's study.

FELLOWSHIPS

Below are listed the endowed fellowships and those paid annually by subscription in the order of their establishment. Special fellowships and such others as have not been noticed in the annual catalogues, are not mentioned

Boudinot Fellowships

Founded in part upon a bequest of the Honorable Elias Boudinot of New Jersey. The invested funds at present amount to eight thousand dollars, and the interest, four hundred dollars, is divided between the Historical and the Modern Language Fellowships. They were established in 1869

Jay Cooke Fellowship in Mathematics

Founded in 1870 and maintained for several years by an annual gift of six hundred dollars from Jay Cooke, Esq , of New York.

Field Fellowship in Classical Literature

Maintained for one year (1870) by a gift of seven hundred dollars from Honorable Richard Stockton Field, of the class of 1821.

Chancellor Green Fellowship in Mental Science

Established in 1870 upon an annual gift of six hundred dollars from Chancellor Henry Woodhull Green, of the class of 1820, and in 1877, after the death of Chancellor Green, endowed by a gift of ten thousand dollars from his widow, Mrs Susan M. Green

Marquand Fellowship in Classical Literature

Established in 1870 and maintained for a number of years by an annual gift of six hundred dollars from Henry G Marquand, Esq., of New York

Class of 1860 Fellowship in Experimental Science

Founded in 1870 upon a gift of ten thousand dollars subscribed by the Class of 1860   A deficiency of income, owing to the depreciation of the value of the securities in which the principal was invested, has been paid from the income of the Magee Professorship of Mining and Engineering, founded by George G Magee, Esq., of the class of 1860

J S K Fellowship in Mathematics

Founded in 1873 upon a gift of eleven thousand dollars from John S. Kennedy, Esq., of New York City   The principal and accumulated interest now amount to sixteen thousand five hundred dollars.

E. M. Biological Fellowship

Founded in 1878.   There is no income to support this fellowship; the present perquisite is the use of a table in the National Seaside Laboratory at Woods Holl, Massachusetts.

Ward Fellowship in Economic Geology

Founded in 1881 by a gift of six hundred dollars from W S. Ward, Esq , of Leadville, Colorado, and awarded in 1882. A like sum, given the following year by Mr. Ward, was offered as a fellowship in Economic Electricity

Fellowship in Chemistry and Mineralogy

The sum of five hundred dollars, given in 1881 by the residuary legatees of John C Green, was offered for one year as a special fellowship in Chemistry and Mineralogy.

Class of 1877 University Fellowship in Biology

Founded in 1887 by members of the Class of 1877 An income of four hundred dollars is paid annually by subscription.

The South East Club University Fellowship in Social Science

Founded in 1887 by alumni of the classes of 1876, 1877, 1878, and 1879—former residents of the South East Entry of Fast College The yearly income of this fellowship, paid partly from invested funds and partly by subscription, amounts to five hundred dollars

University Fellowship in English

Established in 1887 and maintained for a number of years by an annual subscription of four hundred dollars, the gift of Henry M. Alexander, Esq , of the class of 1840, and other gentlemen.

University Fellowship in Archæology

This fellowship, established in 1887, yields an income of four hundred dollars, the annual subscription of several friends of the University.

Fellowships in Oratory

Established in 1891 and maintained for several years by
an annual subscription of twelve hundred dollars, divided into
two fellowships of six hundred dollars each, provided by certain friends of the University.

Thaw Fellowship in Astronomy

Founded in 1897 by a gift of ten thousand dollars from
Mrs Thaw, of Pittsburg.

Charles Scribner University Fellowship in English

Founded in 1899 in memory of Charles Scribner, Esq ,
by his son, Charles Scribner, of the class of 1875, by a gift
of twelve thousand dollars.

John Harding Page Classical Fellowship

Established in 1900 by Mrs James Laughlin, Jr , of Pittsburg, in memory of her father, John Harding Page, Esq.
This fellowship yields the holder the income of six hundred
dollars a year.

Francis Hinton Maule Biological Fellowship

Founded in 1901 by Mr and Mrs Francis Hinton Maule,
as a memorial of their son, Francis Hinton Maule, a student
in the University during the years 1895–1898. The endowment amounts to ten thousand dollars and yields the holder
the annual income of four hundred dollars

ACADEMIC HONORS

1748—1901

PRINCETON UNIVERSITY

ACADEMIC HONORS

1748

Daniel Thane, *Scotland*,   Latin Salutatory[1]

1749

William Burnet, *New Jersey*,   Latin Salutatory

1750[2]

1751

1752

1753

1754

William Shippen, Jr., *Pennsylvania*,   Latin Salutatory

1755

1756

[1] The Latin Salutatory was awarded to the member of the Senior class attaining the highest average in scholarship for the full college course   It still remains the highest honorary appointment at the disposal of the Faculty

[2] No records have been found for the years 1750–53, 1755–59, and 1763–64

1757 [1]

1758

1759

1760

Jonathan Bayard Smith, *Pennsylvania*,	Latin Salutatory
Enoch Green, *New Jersey*,	Valedictory Oration [2]

1761

James Thompson, *New Jersey*,	Latin Salutatory

1762

James Manning, *New Jersey*,	Latin Salutatory
Isaac Allen, *New Jersey*,	Valedictory Oration

1763

1764

1765

Jonathan Edwards, Jr , *Massachusetts*,	Latin Salutatory
Ebenezer Pemberton, *Massachusetts*,	Valedictory Oration

1766

Waightstill Avery, *Connecticut*,	Latin Salutatory
John Haley,	Valedictory Oration

[1] The public exercises of Commencement for this year were omitted, owing
to the illness and death of President Burr, which occurred September 24,
1757 (*Pennsylvania Gazette*, Sept 22, 1757)

[2] The Valedictory oration was awarded with special regard to the qualifications of the student as a valedictorian, as well as on the ground of scholarship   Enoch Green was probably the first undergraduate valedictorian
Prior to this year, at the Commencements of which tnere are records, the Valedictory was delivered by a candidate for the degree of A M , or by a member
of the Faculty

1767

Richard Devens, *Massachusetts,*   Latin Salutatory

1768

Pierpont Edwards, *Massachusetts,*   Latin Salutatory
Isaac Story, *Massachusetts,*   Valedictory Oration

1769

Samuel Stanhope Smith, *Pennsylvania,*   Latin Salutatory
John Henry, *Maryland,*   Valedictory Oration

1770

Nathan Perkins. *Connecticut,*   Latin Salutatory
Robert Stewart, *New York,*   Valedictory Oration

1771[1]

Hugh Henry Brackenridge,[2] *Scotland,*   Latin Salutatory
Gunning Bedford, Jr., *Delaware,*   Valedictory Oration

UNDERGRADUATE PRIZEMEN[3]

ENGLISH   *First,* Aaron Burr, Jr , *New Jersey, Junior;
second,* William Linn, *Pennsylvania, Junior; third,* Belcher Peartree Smith, *New Jersey, Sophomore*

LATIN   Henry Brockholst Livingston, *New Jersey, Freshman, and* David Witherspoon, *New Jersey, Freshman , equal.*

---

[1] James Madison, Jr , of the class of 1771, afterwards fourth President of the United States, was prevented by ill-health, brought on by overwork, from taking any part in the Commencement exercises of this year

[2] Hugh H. Brackenridge also delivered a poem, written conjointly with Philip Freneau, on "The Rising Glory of America," which was printed in Philadelphia the following year (1772) by Joseph Crukshank for R. Aitken, the bookseller.

[3] The competitions for prizes, open to the three lower classes, were held on the day preceding Commencement in the library-room of the College   The first contest occurred in 1771 , the prizemen are given above   The only source for these undergraduate honors being the accounts of the Commencements which appeared in the papers of the day, they are necessarily incomplete

READING LATIN AND GREEK *First*, John Witherspoon, Jr., *New Jersey, Sophomore, second*, Aaron Burr, Jr , *New Jersey, Junior, third*, Henry Lee, Jr , *Virginia, Sophomore*

ENGLISH INTO LATIN Henry Lee, Jr , *Virginia, Sophomore.*

PUBLIC SPEAKING *First*, William Bradford, Jr , *Pennsylvania, Junior, second*, William Linn, *Pennsylvania, Junior, third*, Hugh Hodge, *Pennsylvania, Freshman*

1772[1]

James Grier, *Pennsylvania*,	Latin Salutatory
William Bradford, Jr., *Pennsylvania*,	Valedictory Oration

UNDERGRADUATE PRIZEMEN

ENGLISH *First*, Belcher Peartree Smith, *New Jersey, Junior, second*, John Richardson Bayard Rodgers, *New York, Freshman, third*, John Blair Smith, *Pennsylvania, Junior*

LATIN. *First*, Isaac Stockton Keith, *Pennsylvania, Freshman, second*, John Durbarrow Blair, *New York, Freshman, third*, Charles Lee, *Virginia, Freshman.*

READING LATIN AND GREEK *First*, Samuel Waugh, *Pennsylvania, Junior, second*, John Witherspoon, Jr , *New Jersey, Junior, third*, John Blair Smith, *Pennsylvania, Junior*

ENGLISH INTO LATIN *First*, Samuel Waugh, *Pennsylvania, Junior; second*, Isaac Stockton Keith, *Pennsylvania, Freshman, third*, Daniel Martin, *Pennsylvania, Freshman*

PUBLIC SPEAKING *First*, Jonathan Mason, *Massachusetts, Sophomore, second*, Belcher Peartree Smith, *New Jersey, Junior, third*, Charles Lee, *Virginia, Freshman.*

1773

John Blair Smith, *Pennsylvania*,	Latin Salutatory
Hugh Hodge, *Pennsylvania*,	Valedictory Oration

---

[1] Aaron Burr did not receive either of the high honors upon his graduation in 1772 He delivered a Commencement oration "On Castle-building "

Undergraduate Prizemen

English   *First*, Samuel Leake, Jr., *New Jersey, Junior;*
second, Thomas Harris McCaulle, *North Carolina, Junior.*

Latin.   Charles Lee, *Virginia, Sophomore*

Reading Latin and Greek. *First*, Samuel Leake, Jr,
New Jersey, Junior, second, Thomas Harris McCaulle, *North
Carolina, Junior*

English into Latin.   *First*, Isaac Stockton Keith, *Pennsylvania, Sophomore, second*, Daniel Martin, *Pennsylvania, Sophomore*

Public Speaking.   *First*, Hugh Hodge, *Pennsylvania,
Junior, second*, Charles Lee, *Virginia, Sophomore, third*, John
Richardson Bayard Rodgers, *New York, Sophomore*

1774

Thomas Harris McCaulle, *North Carolina,*   Latin Salutatory[1]
Hugh Hodge,[2] *Pennsylvania,*   Valedictory Oration

Undergraduate Prizemen

English.   *First*, Charles Lee, *Virginia, Junior, second*,
John Richardson Bayard Rodgers, *New York, Junior, third*,
John Durbarrow Blair, *New York, Junior.*

Latin.   *First*, William Ramsay, *Virginia, Sophomore,*
second, Lardner Clark, *New Jersey, Sophomore, third*, John Durbarrow Blair, *New York, Junior*

---

[1] Samuel Leake, Jr , of New Jersey, had been appointed by the Faculty to
deliver the Latin Salutatory in 1774, but the choice was vacated by the Board
of Trustees on the ground that he had been active " in publickly burning the
effigies of his Excellency Governor Hutchinson, and also insulting an honour-
able member of this Board for endeavouring in a very becoming manner to pre-
vent the said riotous proceedings " (*Minutes of the Board of Trustees,* April
19th, 1774.) By this action of the Board, Leake was debarred from any part
in the Commencement exercises, though his merit as a scholar entitled him to
the first honor

[2] A cousin of Hugh Hodge of the preceding class

RFADING LATIN AND GREEK. *First*, Isaac Stockton Keith, *Pennsylvania, Junior, second*, Charles Lee, *Virginia, Junior, third*, William Ramsay, *Virginia, Sophomore.*

ENGLISH INTO LATIN. *First*, William Ramsay, *Virginia, Sophomore, second*, Charles Lee, *Virginia, Junior, third*, Arnold Elzey, *Maryland, Junior*

PUBLIC SPEAKING. *First*, Charles Lee, *Virginia, Junior, second*, John Richardson Bayard Rodgers, *New York, Junior, third*, Benjamin Parker Snowden, *Pennsylvania, Sophomore.*

1775

Charles Lee, *Virginia,*   Latin Salutatory
John Richardson Bayard Rodgers, *New York,*
                                  Valedictory Oration

1776 [1]

1777

1778 [2]

William Boyd, *Pennsylvania,*   First Honorary Oration

1779

George Merchant, *New Jersey,*   Latin Salutatory
Aaron Dickinson Woodruff, *New Jersey,*   Valedictory Oration

---

[1] The Commencement of 1776 was held as usual in September, at Princeton   There is no known record of the proceedings   There were no Commencement exercises or honors assigned in 1777, but the members of the Senior class, seven in number, were subsequently admitted to the degree of A B and are accounted graduates for that year

[2] The members of the Senior class in 1778, were but five in number. The Latin Salutatory oration was pronounced by John Anderson Scudder, of the class of 1775, a candidate for the degree of A M   College orders, interrupted by the invasion of New Jersey by the British, and the damage resulting to the College property from its occupation by both armies, were not resumed until 1778, save in the most desultory manner, as the exigencies of the war permitted

1780

Samuel W Venable, *Virginia*,	Latin Salutatory
James Roosevelt, *New York*,	Valedictory Oration

1781

Joseph Clark, *New Jersey*,	Latin Salutatory
Robert Smith, *Pennsylvania*,	Valedictory Oration

1782

William Mahon, *Virginia*,	Latin Salutatory
John Morton, *New York*,	Valedictory Oration

1783

Obadiah Holmes, *New Jersey*,	Latin Salutatory
Ashbel Green, *New Jersey*,	Valedictory Oration

COMPETITIVE ORATIONS[1]

Cliosophic Society

Gilbert Tennent Snowden, *Pennsylvania*,	*Senior*

American Whig Society

Ashbel Green, *New Jersey*,	*Senior*

1784

Joseph Clay, *Georgia*,	Latin Salutatory
James Asheton Bayard, *Pennsylvania*,	English Salutatory
Samuel Bayard, *Pennsylvania*,	Valedictory Oration

DICKINSON MEDAL[2]

Joseph Clay,	*Georgia*

[1] This was the first public competition between the two Literary Societies The orations were delivered on the Fourth of July, 1783, before a large and brilliant audience, which included the Congress of the United States, then assembled at Princeton See Giger's *History of the Chosophic Society*, p 87.

[2] John Dickinson, Esq , Governor of Delaware, presented to the Board of Trustees, in 1782, his note for £100, proposing that the "interest of so much of it as the Trustees may judge proper, might annually, or as often as they

Competitive Orations[1]

Chosophic Society

Joseph Clay, *Georgia,*   *Senior*

American Whig Society

James Asheton Bayard, *Pennsylvania,*   *Senior*

Undergraduate Prizemen

ENGLISH. *First,* Samuel Finley Snowden, *Pennsylvania, Sophomore, second,* Thomas Pollock, *North Carolina, Sophomore, third,* Hercules Whaley, *New York, Junior.*

LATIN GRAMMAR *First,* John Wright Vancleve, *New Jersey, Sophomore, second,* Lucius Horatio Stockton, *New Jersey, Freshman*

ENGLISH AND LATIN VERSIONS Robert Goodloe Harper, *Virginia, Junior*

ENGLISH ORATIONS *First,* Lucius Horatio Stockton, *New Jersey, Freshman, second,* Maturin Livingston, *New York, Sophomore, third,* Hercules Whaley, *New York, Junior*

1785

James McCoy, *North Carolina,*   Latin Salutatory
Oliver L Ker, *New York,*   Valedictory Oration

Undergraduate Prizemen[2]

ENGLISH. *First,* Edward Graham, *North Carolina, Junior,*

approve, be applied in procuring a gold or silver medal to be bestowed upon the student who shall compose the best dissertation on some of the following subjects " (*Minutes of the Board of Trustees,* Sept 25, 1782) Only one dissertation being presented in 1783, the subject was republished and no award made until the following year The awards were discontinued after 1789 from a lack of interest among the students, and not again revived until 1872 This was the first endowed prize offered by the College, and is well-known at the present day

[1] Delivered at the Commencement, Sept 29, 1784

[2] Dickinson medal not awarded

second, William King Hugg, *New Jersey, Junior, third*, Samuel Finley Snowden, *Pennsylvania, Junior.*

ENGLISH ORATIONS   *First*, Lucius Horatio Stockton, *New Jersey, Sophomore, second*, George Clarkson, *Pennsylvania, Freshman, third*, John Wright Vancleve, *New Jersey, Junior*

1786

Samuel Finley Snowden, *Pennsylvania*,	Latin Salutatory
Edward Johnston, *Maryland*,	Second Latin Salutatory
Maturin Livingston, *New York*,	Valedictory Oration

1787

Nathaniel Higginson, *Massachusetts*,	Latin Salutatory
Evan Alexander, *North Carolina*,	Greek Salutatory
Lucius Horatio Stockton, *New Jersey*,	Valedictory Oration

DICKINSON MEDAL

Nathaniel Higginson,	*Massachusetts*

UNDERGRADUATE PRIZEMEN

ENGLISH.   *First*, Richard Randolph, *Virginia, Sophomore, second*, Edward Darrell, *South Carolina, Sophomore, third*, George Clarkson, *Pennsylvania, Junior.*

LATIN   *First*, David Deas, *South Carolina, Sophomore, second*, Silas Wood, *New York, Sophomore, third*, Barak Gibbons, *Freshman*

ENGLISH ORATIONS.   *First*, Richard Randolph, *Virginia, Sophomore, second*, Henry Deas, *South Carolina, Sophomore, third*, Thomas Young, *South Carolina, Freshman.*

1788

David Stone, *North Carolina*,	Latin Salutatory
Nicholas Van Dycke, *Delaware*,	English Salutatory
George Clarkson, *Pennsylvania*,	Valedictory Oration

UNDERGRADUATE PRIZEMEN

ENGLISH   *First,* David Deas, *South Carolina, Junior;
second,* Charles Snowden, *Pennsylvania, Junior, third,* Nathaniel Boileau, *Pennsylvania, Junior.*

LATIN   *First,* David Deas, *South Carolina, Junior, second,* Thomas Young, *South Carolina, Sophomore*

ENGLISH INTO LATIN.   William Johnson, *South Carolina, Sophomore.*

ENGLISH ORATIONS.   *First,* Benjamin F. Timothy, *Sophomore, second,* David Deas, *South Carolina, Junior, third,* Isaac Watts Crane, *New Jersey, Junior*

1789

Silas Wood, *New York,*	Latin Salutatory
Charles Snowden, *Pennsylvania,*	English Salutatory
David Deas, *South Carolina,*	Valedictory Oration

1790

William Johnson, *South Carolina,*	Latin Salutatory
John Taylor, *South Carolina,*	English Salutatory
Ezekiel Pickens, *South Carolina,*	Valedictory Oration

UNDERGRADUATE PRIZEMEN

ENGLISH.   *First,* Joseph Caldwell, *New Jersey, Junior, second,* Frederick Stone, *Maryland, Junior; third,* Peter Wykoff, *New Jersey, Junior.*

ENGLISH ORATIONS   *First,* Joseph Reed, *Pennsylvania, Sophomore, second,* James C. Roosevelt, *New York, Junior, third,* Edmund Jennings Lee, *Virginia, Sophomore;* Francis Markoe, *West Indies, Junior; fifth,* Ebenezer Rhea, *Pennsylvania, Junior, sixth,* Abraham Skinner, *New York, Freshman.*

1791

Joseph Caldwell, *New Jersey,*	Latin Salutatory
James C Roosevelt, *New York,*	English Salutatory
Jacob Burnet, *New Jersey,*	Mathematical Oration

Ebenezer Rhea, *Pennsylvania,*   Honorary Oration
Peter Wykoff, *New Jersey,*   Valedictory Oration

UNDERGRADUATE PRIZEMEN

ENGLISH. *First,* Joseph Reed, *Pennsylvania, Junior, second,* George Washington Morton, *New York, Junior; third,* Edmund Jennings Lee, *Virginia, Junior.*

ENGLISH ORATIONS *First,* Joseph Reed, *Pennsylvania, Junior, second,* Edmund Jennings Lee, *Virginia, Junior; third,* John Witherspoon Smith, *New Jersey, Freshman.*

1792

Alexander White, *Virginia,*   Latin Salutatory
Peter Early, *Virginia,*   English Salutatory
Charles Wilson Harris, *North Carolina,*   Mathematical Oration
Joseph Reed, *Pennsylvania,*   Valedictory Oration
John Conrad Otto, *New Jersey,*   Honorary Oration
Edmund Jennings Lee, *Virginia,*   Honorary Oration

1793

John Henry Hobart,[1] *Pennsylvania,*   Latin Salutatory
Bennet Taylor, *Virginia,*   English Salutatory
Robert Hunt, *New Jersey,*   Belles Lettres Oration
John Gibson, *Pennsylvania,*   Mathematical Oration
Abraham Skinner, *New York,*   Valedictory Oration
Robert Ogden, *New Jersey,*   Honorary Oration
Joshua Maddox Wallace, *New Jersey,*   Honorary Oration
John Terhune, *New York,*   Honorary Oration

1794

Thomas Yardley How, *New Jersey,*   Latin Salutatory
Titus Hutchinson, *Vermont,*   English Salutatory
John Bradford Wallace, *New Jersey,*   Valedictory Oration

[1] The merit of Hobart and Taylor was considered equal and their choice of orations determined by lot. *Minutes of the Faculty,* July 15, 1793

George Washington Campbell, *North Carolina,*
                                 Mathematical Oration

Richard M Green, *New Jersey,*	Honorary Oration
James M. Broom, *Delaware,*	Honorary Oration
John Sylvanus Hiester, *Pennsylvania,*	Honorary Oration

1795

George G Bowie, *South Carolina,*	Latin Salutatory
Robert Johnstone Taylor, *Virginia,*	English Salutatory
Edward Darrell Smith, *South Carolina,*	Valedictory Oration
John Sergeant, *Pennsylvania,*	Mathematical Oration
Thomas Brown, *New Jersey,*	Belles Lettres Oration
Silas Condict, *New Jersey,*	Honorary Oration
Samuel Hayes, *New Jersey,*	Honorary Oration
George Clark Morton, *New York,*	Honorary Oration

UNDERGRADUATE PRIZEMEN

ENGLISH ORATIONS *First,* Robert Marshall Forsyth, *Georgia, Junior; second,* Elias Boudinot Caldwell, *New Jersey, Junior, third,* Joseph Reed, *New York, Junior*

1796

William Gaston, *North Carolina,*	Latin Salutatory
Philip Clayton Pendleton, *Virginia,*	English Salutatory
Robert Marshall Forsyth, *Georgia,*	Valedictory Oration
Moses J Cantine, *New York,*	Honorary Oration
John Fitzgerald, *Virginia,*	Honorary Oration
Joseph Blount Littlejohn, *North Carolina,*	Honorary Oration
Nathaniel Venable, *Virginia,*	Honorary Oration

1797

Charles Fenton Mercer, *Virginia,*	Latin Salutatory
Peter Le Conte, *New Jersey,*	English Salutatory
James W. Clarke, *North Carolina,*	Valedictory Oration
Frederick Beasley, *North Carolina,*	Belles Lettres Oration
Thomas Bayley, *Maryland,*	Mathematical Oration

Henry Waggaman Edwards,[1] *Connecticut,*   Honorary Oration
John Howe Peyton, *Virginia,*   Honorary Oration
John Stoops, *Maryland,*   Honorary Oration

1798

Charles Ewing, *New Jersey,*   Latin Salutatory
Thomas Sergeant, *Pennsylvania,*   Valedictory Oration
Henry Sergeant, *Pennsylvania,*   English Salutatory
Benjamin B Hopkins,[2] *New York,*   Mathematical Oration
Josiah Watson, *Virginia,*   Belles Lettres Oration
Theodore F. Talbot, *New York,*   Honorary Oration
George W. Jackson, *Maryland,*   Honorary Oration
Edward Hugh Jones, *Pennsylvania,*   Honorary Oration
John Van Artsdalen, *Pennsylvania,*   Honorary Oration

1799

Thomas Miller, *Virginia,*   Latin Salutatory
Henry G Wisner, *New York,*   Valedictory Oration
Frederick Nash, *North Carolina,*   English Salutatory
James Cathcart Johnson, *North Carolina,* Belles Lettres Oration
John Van Dyke, *New Jersey,*   Mathematical Oration
Isaac Meason,[3] *Pennsylvania,*   Honorary Oration
John Forsyth, *Georgia,*   Honorary Oration
James Rogers, *Delaware,*   Honorary Oration

1800

Philemon Hunt, *New Jersey,*   Latin Salutatory
James Carnahan, *Pennsylvania,*   English Salutatory
Arthur Rose Fitzhugh, *Virginia,*   Valedictory Oration
George Mifflin, *Pennsylvania,*   Belles Lettres Oration
William A. Gregory, *Virginia,*   Mathematical Oration

---

[1] The scholarship of Edwards, Peyton, and Stoops was considered equal *Minutes of the Faculty,* August 16, 1797

[2] Hopkins and Watson adjudged equal in scholarship *Ibid,* Sept 12, 1798

[3] Meason, Forsyth, and Rogers of equal scholarship *Ibid,* Sept 12, 1799

1801

Edward D. Watts,[1] *Virginia*,	Latin Salutatory
Nicholas Biddle, *Pennsylvania*,	Valedictory Oration
Henry Edward Watkins, *Virginia*,	English Salutatory
John Grattan Gamble, *Virginia*,	Mathematical Oration
James Crommelin, *New Jersey*,	Belles Lettres Oration
Elias E Ellmaker, *Pennsylvania*,	Honorary Oration
John McDowell, *New Jersey*,	Honorary Oration
William Bell Paterson, *New Jersey*,	Honorary Oration

1802

George Emlen, *Pennsylvania*,	Latin Salutatory
John Purdon, *Pennsylvania*,	English Salutatory
William McIlvaine, Jr., *New Jersey*,	Valedictory Oration
Richard H Henderson, *Virginia*,	Belles Lettres Oration
Robert Habersham, *Georgia*,	Mathematical Oration
David Allen, *Virginia*,	Honorary Oration
George Strawbridge, *Delaware*,	Honorary Oration
Hext McCall, *South Carolina*,	Honorary Oration

UNDERGRADUATE ORATIONS[2]

Cliosophic Society

Alfred Cuthbert, *Georgia*,	*Junior*
John Dowman Edwards, *South Carolina*,	*Junior*
George Meason, *Pennsylvania*,	*Sophomore*
Josiah Simpson, *Pennsylvania*,	*Junior*

[1] Scholarship of Watts and Biddle considered equal, as also was that of Gamble and Crommelin *Minutes of the Faculty*, Sept 10, 1801

[2] "On the preceding evening (Tuesday, Sept 28, 1802) the following young gentlemen, previously appointed by the two literary societies in the College, for that purpose, pronounced orations in the church" (*Trenton Federalist*, Oct 18, 1802) This is an early and isolated instance of competition between the two Societies by four representatives from each, on the evening preceding Commencement day This custom was not regularly instituted until several years later, when it became known as the "Junior Commencement," the Junior Orations of the present day

American Whig Society

Robert C Brown, *Maryland*,	*Junior*
Joseph Reed Ingersoll, *Pennsylvania*,	*Sophomore*
Paul S H. Lee, *South Carolina*,	*Sophomore*
Thomas Marshall, *Virginia*,	*Junior*

1803

William Hay,[1] *Virginia*,	Latin Salutatory
John Ralph, *Maryland*,	English Salutatory
Thomas Marshall, *Virginia*,	Valedictory Oration
Alfred Cuthbert, *Georgia*,	Belles Lettres Oration
John Miller, *Virginia*,	Mathematical Oration
Comegys Paul, *New Jersey*,	Historical Oration
William Neill, *Pennsylvania*,	Honorary Oration
Severyn Bruyn, *New York*,	Honorary Oration
David Thompson, *New Jersey*,	Honorary Oration

1804

Joseph Reed Ingersoll, *Pennsylvania*,	Latin Salutatory
Jacob R. Theodore Frelinghuysen, *New Jersey*,	
	Valedictory Oration
William W Wilson, *Maryland*,	English Salutatory
Philip Holbrook Nicklin, *Pennsylvania*,	Mathematical Oration
Samuel Lewis Southard, *New Jersey*,	Theological Oration
Charles Wilkins, *Pennsylvania*,	Moral Science Oration
Elihu Spencer Sergeant, *Pennsylvania*,	Physical Science Oration
George Poyntell, *Pennsylvania*,	Belles Lettres Oration
George Chambers, *Pennsylvania*,	Historical Oration
Thomas Hartley Crawford, *Pennsylvania*,	
	Political Science Oration

1805

Hezekiah Belknap, *New York*,	Latin Salutatory
John R Crane, *New Jersey*,	English Salutatory

---

[1] The scholarship of Hay and Ralph of equal merit, as also was that of Miller and Paul. *Minutes of the Faculty*, Sept 8, 1803

John Morin Scott, *Pennsylvania,*   Valedictory Oration
Amos S Ellmaker, *Pennsylvania,*   Mathematical Oration
John A Cuthbert, *Georgia,*   Theological Oration
St Leger Landon Carter, *Virginia,*   Moral Science Oration
Hooper Cumming, *New Jersey,*   Belles Lettres Oration
William Clay Cumming, *Georgia,*   Physical Science Oration
Wright C Stanley, *North Carolina,*   Historical Oration
James Montgomery, *Pennsylvania,*   Political Science Oration
William Conover Schenck, *New Jersey,*   Classical Oration

1806

John James Marshall, *Kentucky,*   Latin Salutatory
John Eager Howard, *Maryland,*   English Salutatory
Rider H Winder, *Maryland,*   Valedictory Oration
Lewis Le Conte Congar, *New Jersey,*   Mathematical Oration
John Croes, *New Jersey,*   Theological Oration
George Read, *Delaware,*   Moral Science Oration
John Williams Walker, *Georgia,*   Belles Lettres Oration
Edward Colston, *Virginia,*   Historical Oration
Israel Peyton Thompson, *Virginia,*   Physical Science Oration
James Iredell, *North Carolina,*   Political Science Oration
Patrick Noble, *South Carolina,*   Classical Literature Oration

1807

Thomson Mason,[1] *Virginia,*   Latin Salutatory
James King, *New York,*   Valedictory Oration
Alem Marr, *Pennsylvania,*   English Salutatory
John Handley, *New Jersey,*   Mathematical Oration
George W Brown, *Pennsylvania,*   Belles Lettres Oration
Daniel Harrison Condict, *New Jersey,*   Moral Science Oration
Isaac R Marshall, *Pennsylvania,*   Physical Science Oration
Charles Edwin Pierson, *New Jersey,*   Historical Oration

---

[1] Thomson Mason was appointed Latin Salutatorian by the Faculty, but to oblige his class pronounced the Valedictory Oration, exchanging places with James King, who then delivered the Latin Salutatory   *Trenton Federalist,* Oct 12, 1807

1808

William Henry Fitzhugh,[1] *Virginia*,	Latin Salutatory
William Meade, *Virginia*,	Valedictory Oration
George Wood, *New Jersey*,	English Salutatory
Elijah Slack, *Pennsylvania*,	Philosophical Oration
John M Verdier, *South Carolina*,	Moral Science Oration
William G Ernst, *Pennsylvania*,	Theological Oration
George King Drake, *New Jersey*,	Mathematical Oration
Richard Smith Coxe, *New Jersey*,	Belles Lettres Oration
Thomas F Herbert, *Virginia*,	Historical Oration
Daniel A. Clark, *New Jersey*,	Classical Literature Oration
William Montgomery, *Pennsylvania*,	Political Science Oration

1809

George W Cook, *North Carolina*,	Latin Salutatory
Jacob Gray Macwhorter, *South Carolina*,	English Salutatory
Benjamin Chew Howard, *Maryland*,	Valedictory Oration

HONORARY SENIOR ORATIONS[2]

Franklin Anderson,	*Maryland*
Charles E. Brown,	*Louisiana*
John De Witt,	*New York*
Samuel W Eager,	*New York*
William Finney,	*Pennsylvania*
Ezekiel Forman,	*Maryland*
William Anderson McDowell,	*New Jersey*
Thomas Coxe Ryerson,	*New Jersey*
Thomas Harvey Skinner,	*North Carolina*
Thomas Turner Stanley,	*North Carolina*

[1] Fitzhugh, Meade, and Wood of equal rank   *Minutes of the Faculty*, Sept 4, 1808

[2] The minutes of the Faculty being deficient for the years 1809–1812, inclusive, the names of those who delivered honorary orations, other than the three highest honors, have been alphabetically arranged under this group, as their relative standing can not be determined   These orations indicate high standing   The honors for this period are compiled from the published accounts of the Commencements which appeared in the contemporary papers

William Raymond Weeks, *New York,*   Greek Oration
John Wiley,   *District of Columbia*
John S Wood,   *New Jersey*

1810

Jared D. Fyler, *New York,*   Latin Salutatory
John T Stoddert, *District of Columbia,*   English Salutatory
George Mifflin Dallas, *Pennsylvania,*   Valedictory Oration

HONORARY SENIOR ORATIONS

James C. Baldwin,   *New Jersey*
Robert Bronk,   *New York*
Andrew De Witte Bruyn,   *New York*
Horace Galpin,   *New York*
Oliver Spencer Halsted,   *New Jersey*
Matthias Ogden,   *New Jersey*
William T Read,   *Delaware*

UNDERGRADUATE ORATIONS[1]

Cliosophic Society

Thomas G Haight, *Pennsylvania,*   *Sophomore*
John Thompson, *Delaware,*   *Sophomore*
Isaac Ward, *New Jersey,*   *Junior*

American Whig Society

John Boykin, *South Carolina,*   *Junior*
Samuel L. Holmes, *New York,*   *Junior*
Edward E. Lawrence, *New York,*   *Sophomore*
William States Lee, *South Carolina*   *Sophomore*

1811

William Francis Taliaferro, *Virginia,*   Latin Salutatory
Singleton Wooton, *Maryland,*   English Salutatory
James Dunlop, *District of Columbia,*   Valedictory Oration

[1] The *Trenton Federalist* states (Oct 8, 1810) that these orators were "chosen by their fellow students from among the inferior classes in the college "

Honorary Senior Orations[1]

Lewis Belden, *Connecticut,*	Theology
John Boykin, *South Carolina,*	Belles Lettres
Isaac Gouverneur, *New York,*	Mathematics
Nicholas Gouverneur, *New York,*	History
John Hopkins, *Virginia,*	Philosophy

Undergraduate Orations

Cliosophic Society

Cyrus Gildersleeve, Jr , *Georgia,*	*Junior*
Thomas G Haight, *Pennsylvania,*	*Junior*
Mordecai Myers, *South Carolina,*	*Junior*
John Thompson, *Delaware,*	*Junior*

American Whig Society

Thomas Bloomer Balch, *District of Columbia,*	*Sophomore*
Edward E Lawrence, *New York,*	*Junior*
William States Lee, *South Carolina,*	*Junior*
Samuel J Wilkin, *New York,*	*Junior*

1812

Brice W. Howard, *Maryland,*	Latin Salutatory
John S Haines, *Pennsylvania,*	English Salutatory
William Fanning Wickham, *Virginia,*	Valedictory Oration

Honorary Senior Orations

John Ford, *New Jersey,*	Latin
Cyrus Gildersleeve, Jr., *Georgia,*	Theology
John Henderson, *Pennsylvania,*	Mathematics
Levi Janvier, *Delaware,*	Classics
George H Macwhorter, *New Jersey,*	Moral Science
Benjamin Whitemarsh Seabrook, *South Carolina,*	Philosophy
Nicholas Van Dyke, Jr , *Delaware,*	History

[1] Orations " in testimony of honorable proficiency " in the several sciences.
Trenton Federalist, Sept 30, 1811

1813

First Honor[1]

Thomas Chapman, *New Jersey*,	Valedictory Oration
Aaron Ogden Dayton, *New Jersey*,	English Salutatory
Samuel Jaudon, *Pennsylvania*,	Philosophical Oration
John Wurts, *Pennsylvania*,	Latin Salutatory

Second Honor

William Howe Cuyler, *Georgia*,	Political Science Oration
Amzi Dodd, *New Jersey*,	Mathematical Oration
Joseph Smith Dodd, *New Jersey*,	Theological Oration
John B Downman, *Virginia*,	Moral Science Oration
Robert Peter Dunlop, *District of Columbia*,	
	Classical Literature Oration
Joseph W Helme, *New York*,	Historical Oration
Edward Young Howell, *Pennsylvania*,	Belles Lettres Oration

1814

First Honor[2]

John Blair Dabney, *Virginia*,	Latin Salutatory
Hugh Lenox Hodge, *Pennsylvania*,	Moral Science Oration
Bloomfield McIlvaine, *New Jersey*,	Valedictory Oration
Stephen Saunders, *Connecticut*,	English Salutatory

[1] The Faculty decided that Chapman, Dayton, Jaudon, and Wurts were equally entitled to the first honor, and that Cuyler, A Dodd, J S Dodd, Downman, Dunlop, Helme, and Howell were equally entitled to the second The choice of orations in each group was determined by lot. (*Minutes of the Faculty*, Sept. 1, 1813) The names are alphabetically arranged, as has been done in all cases where the appointment was decided by lot The Presbyterian church in which Commencement was annually held, had been destroyed by fire in February of this year (1813), and had not then been rebuilt, and for lack of a suitable building the public exercises were omitted

[2] Dabney, Saunders, McIlvaine, and Hodge were considered by the Faculty equally entitled to the first honor The choice of orations was determined by lot *Minutes of the Faculty*, August 29, 1814

Second Honor

William W. Miller, *New Jersey,*   Belles Lettres Oration

Third Honor

Melancthon B. Williams, *New Jersey,* Historical Oration

Fourth Honor[1]

William Mayo Atkinson, *Virginia,* Political Science Oration
Henry Carrington, *Virginia,*   Oration on Chemistry
Robert Woodruff Condit, *New Jersey,*
         Classical Literature Oration
Horace Cozens, *District of Columbia,* Philosophical Oration
Lemuel Fordham Leake, *New Jersey,* Sacred Literature Oration
Jonathan Price, *New Jersey,*   Mathematical Oration

Undergraduate Prizemen

Mathematics Elijah Richardson Craven, *District of Columbia, Junior, and* Enos W. Johnson, *New York, Junior, equal for first honor,* Persifer Frazer Smith, *Pennsylvania, Junior, and* Charles Samuel Stewart, *New Jersey, Junior, equal for second honor.*

English Composition. Philip Ricard Fendall, *Virginia, Junior.*

Reading English Edward Allen, *Connecticut, Junior*

Geography John Smith Newbold, *Pennsylvania, Sophomore, and* John Taylor, *Virginia, Sophomore, equal*

Latin Joseph A. Hamilton, *New Jersey, Freshman, and* Samuel Stiles, *Georgia, Freshman, equal.*

---

[1] Atkinson, Carrington, Condit, Leake, Cozens, and Price equally entitled to fourth honor. *Minutes of the Faculty,* August 29, 1814

1815

First Honor [1]

Philip Ricard Fendall, *Virginia*,	Latin Salutatory
John Johns, *Delaware*,	English Salutatory

Second Honor

Charles Hodge, *Pennsylvania*,	Theological Oration
Alexander Wurts, *Pennsylvania*,	Valedictory Oration

Third Honor

Charles Samuel Stewart, *New Jersey*,	Belles Lettres Oration

Fourth Honor

Edward Allen, *Connecticut*,	Political Science Oration
Lawrence Battaile, *Virginia*,	Honorary Oration
Elijah Richardson Craven, *District of Columbia*,	
	Classical Literature Oration

Fifth Honor

Daniel Baker, *Georgia*,	Mathematical Oration
Thomas Jacob Biggs, *Pennsylvania*,	Honorary Oration
Robert I. Clarke, *Pennsylvania*,	Honorary Oration

Undergraduate Prizemen [2]

English Composition. Robert Allen Jones, *North Carolina, Junior.*

English Grammar. Eli Washington Caruthers, *North Carolina, Sophomore.*

Latin Samuel Fisher Darrach, *Pennsylvania, Freshman.*

---

[1] Names under each honor group are equally entitled to such honors, the choice of orations was determined as usual by lot. *Minutes of the Faculty,* August 7–16, 1815

[2] " It was resolved that the names of the successful competitors be mentioned publickly on the day of commencement, and it was likewise resolved that a book be presented to each victorious competitor in testimony of his

1816

First Honor[1]

James Cox, *Pennsylvania*,   Moral Science Oration
Samuel Cox, *Pennsylvania*,   Mathematical Oration
James McDowell, *Virginia*,   Latin Salutatory
John Smith Newbold, *Pennsylvania*,   Belles Lettres Oration
Albert Pierson, *New Jersey*,   Valedictory Oration
William Pierson, *New Jersey*,   English Salutatory
Richard Renshaw Thomson, *Pennsylvania*,
                                    Classical Literature Oration

Second Honor

William Jessup Armstrong, *New Jersey*,   Honorary Oration
Amzi Babbitt, *New Jersey*,   Honorary Oration
George Washington Toland, *Pennsylvania*,   Honorary Oration

Third Honor

John Rodney, *Delaware*,   Honorary Oration

Fourth Honor

Littleton James Dennis, *Maryland*,   Honorary Oration
Charles Pettit McIlvaine, *New Jersey*,   Honorary Oration
Kensey Johns Van Dyke, *Delaware*,   Honorary Oration

success." (*Minutes of the Faculty*, Sept 27, 1814) The competitions in
Mathematics, English Composition, and the reading of English were confined
to the members of the Junior class, those in Geography, to the Sophomore
class, and those in Latin, to the Freshman class Undergraduate competitions were discontinued after the fall of 1815, and were not revived until 1873,
except with respect to the orations delivered the evening before Commencement. There is no record of any competition between 1791 and 1814 See
Maclean's *History of the College of New Jersey*, II, 161.

[1] Names under each group are equally entitled to such honors and are
alphabetically arranged   Those in the first and second groups were assigned
orations by lot, the others were allowed to select their own subjects *Minutes
of the Faculty*, August 5–13, 1816

FIFTH HONOR

Robert Allen Jones, *North Carolina*,	Honorary Oration
John Maclean, *New Jersey*,	Honorary Oration

SIXTH HONOR

Isaac Washington Canfield, *New Jersey*,	Honorary Oration
James Van Lear, *Maryland*,	Honorary Oration

1817

FIRST HONOR

John Van Lear McMahon, *Maryland*,	Latin Salutatory

SECOND HONOR

Benjamin Ogden, *New Jersey*,	English Salutatory

THIRD HONOR

George McDowell Stroud, *Pennsylvania*,	Valedictory Oration

FOURTH HONOR

John Harriotte Van Court, *New Jersey*,	Honorary Oration

FIFTH HONOR[1]

William B Barton, *New Jersey*,	Honorary Oration
Chester Butler, *Pennsylvania*,	Honorary Oration
John J Pierce, *New York*	Honorary Oration
Robert C. Hall, *Pennsylvania*,	Honorary Oration
Aaron Samuel Pennington, *New Jersey*,	Honorary Oration

SIXTH HONOR

John L. Baldwin, *New Jersey*,	Honorary Oration
Eli Washington Caruthers, *North Carolina*,	Honorary Oration
John S Condit, *New Jersey*,	Honorary Oration

[1] Those under the fifth and sixth honor groups equally entitled to such honors *Minutes of the Faculty*, August 6, 1817

Edmund Jennings Lee, *Virginia*,   Honorary Oration
John Vanderveer, *New Jersey*,   Honorary Oration

1818

FIRST HONOR

Joseph McIlvaine, *New Jersey*,   Latin Salutatory

SECOND HONOR[1]

Stephen Collins,   *Maryland*
John R Montgomery, *Pennsylvania*,   English Salutatory

THIRD HONOR

John Breckinridge, *Kentucky*,   Honorary Oration

FOURTH HONOR

Joseph Chambers, *Pennsylvania*,   Honorary Oration
James Hunter Ewing, *Pennsylvania*,   Honorary Oration
Philip Courtlandt Hay, *New Jersey*,   Honorary Oration
William H Roy, *Virginia*,   Honorary Oration

FIFTH HONOR

Samuel Fisher Darrach, *Pennsylvania*,   Honorary Oration
Archibald Irwin Findlay, *Pennsylvania*,   Honorary Oration
George W. Neff, *Pennsylvania*,   Honorary Oration
George Washington Smith, *Pennsylvania*,   Honorary Oration
Abraham Williamson, *New Jersey*,   Honorary Oration

SIXTH HONOR

Cornelius L. Allen, *New York*,   Honorary Oration
Daniel Theodore Coxe, *Pennsylvania*,   Honorary Oration
Charles S W Dorsey, *Maryland*,   Honorary Oration
Josiah Bertram Howell, *New Jersey*,   Honorary Oration

---

[1] Those under each group considered of equal standing   *Minutes of the Faculty*, August 10, 1818

Seventh Honor

David Barrow, *Tennessee*,	Honorary Oration
John Joseph Chetwood, *New Jersey*,	Honorary Oration
Thomas F. McCaleb, *Mississippi*,	Honorary Oration

1819

First Honor[1]

John Charles Groome, *Maryland*,	Honorary Oration
John Izard Middleton, *South Carolina*,	Latin Salutatory
John Frederick Schroeder, *Maryland*,	English Salutatory

Second Honor

Joseph Henry Lumpkin, *Georgia*,	Honorary Oration

Third Honor

William Lyle McDowell, *Virginia*,	Honorary Oration
Elias Bailey Dayton Ogden, *New Jersey*,	Honorary Oration
Andrew Walker, *Pennsylvania*,	Honorary Oration

Fourth Honor

Benjamin Franklin Bache, *New Jersey*,	Honorary Oration
Thomas Jefferson Lumpkin, *Georgia*,	Honorary Oration
Abraham Woodson Venable, *Virginia*,	Honorary Oration
Stephen Dodd Ward, *New Jersey*,	Honorary Oration

Fifth Honor

Henry King Cochran, *Virginia*,	Honorary Oration
John Berkley Grimball, *South Carolina*,	Honorary Oration
James McIlhany, *Virginia*,	Honorary Oration
James Ross, *Maryland*,	Honorary Oration
John Allan Stuart, *South Carolina*,	Valedictory Oration
John Townsend, *South Carolina*,	Honorary Oration
William Baily Tyler, *Virginia*,	Honorary Oration
Hugh Wilson, *North Carolina*,	Honorary Oration

[1] Those under each honor group equal in scholarship *Minutes of the Faculty*, August 9, 1819

Sixth Honor

Jacob Hay, Jr , *Pennsylvania,*	Honorary Oration
Holloway Whitefield Hunt, Jr , *New Jersey,*	Honorary Oration
Abraham Skillman, *New Jersey,*	Honorary Oration
Elias Van Arsdale, Jr., *New Jersey,*	Honorary Oration

1820

First Honor

James Bayard, *Pennsylvania,*	Honorary Oration
John Thompson Brown, *Virginia,*	English Salutatory
William Perroneau Finley, *South Carolina,*	Latin Salutatory

Second Honor

William Mumford Carter, *Virginia,*	Honorary Oration
James H Gholson, *Virginia,*	Valedictory Oration
Henry Woodhull Green, *New Jersey,*	Honorary Oration

Third Honor

Clement Cox, *District of Columbia,*	Honorary Oration
James Caldwell Finley, *New Jersey,*	Honorary Oration
Alfred Iverson, *Georgia,*	Honorary Oration
William George Krebs, *Pennsylvania,*	Honorary Oration
George Washington Massey, *Maryland,*	Honorary Oration
Province McCormick, *Virginia,*	Honorary Oration

Fourth Honor

Richard Bard, *Pennsylvania,*	Honorary Oration
William Ludwell Hodgson, *District of Columbia,*	
	Honorary Oration
Henry M Read, *Pennsylvania,*	Honorary Oration

[1] Those under each group equal in scholarship   (*Minutes of the Faculty,* August 7, 1820) The minutes of the Faculty from August 27, 1820, until November 12, 1835, are missing   The honors for this period are collated from the newspapers of New Jersey

George Bridges Rodney, *Delaware,*   Honorary Oration
Allison Ross, *Mississippi,*   Honorary Oration
Samuel Kennedy Talmage, *New Jersey,*   Honorary Oration

Fifth Honor

George W. Blight, *New Jersey,*   Honorary Oration
Harvey Lindsly, *New Jersey,*   Honorary Oration
Ebenezer Mason, *New York,*   Honorary Oration
Alexander Mazyck, *South Carolina,*   Honorary Oration
Edward Thomas, *New Jersey,*   Honorary Oration
William Walker, *Virginia,*   Honorary Oration

Sixth Honor

James Waddell Alexander, *Virginia,*   Honorary Oration
William Brearly, *New Jersey,*   Honorary Oration
Thomas Chambers, *Pennsylvania,*   Honorary Oration
John V Garritson, *New Jersey,*   Honorary Oration
James Bailey Hyndshaw, *New Jersey,*   Honorary Oration
Benjamin E Ward, *New York,*   Honorary Oration

1821

William Schley, *Maryland,*   Latin Salutatory
Alexander Aikman, *New Jersey,*   English Salutatory

Honorary Orations[1]

Richard Stockton Field, *New Jersey,*   Valedictory Oration
Robert Smith Finley,   *New Jersey*
Robert Porterfield Augustus Heiskell,   *Virginia*
David Jenkins,   *Pennsylvania*
William Bainbridge Maclean,   *New Jersey*
John D Read,   *Delaware*

[1] As there is no official record of the honors for the years 1821 to 1835, the minutes of the Faculty being deficient for that period, a complete list of the honorary orations delivered at Commencement, other than the two highest honors, is given in alphabetical order, as their relative standing cannot be determined

Moses Coleman Searle,   *Massachusetts*
George Archibald Smith,   *District of Columbia*
Alfred Augustus Sowers,   *Virginia*
James H Stuart,   *Pennsylvania*

1822

Edward Deering Mansfield, *New York*,   Latin Salutatory
Hugh Mearns, *Pennsylvania*,   English Salutatory

HONORARY ORATIONS

William S Buchanan,   *Pennsylvania*
Thomas W. Clymer,   *Pennsylvania*
William W Deneale,   *Virginia*
Jacoby De Pui,   *Pennsylvania*
Philemon Dickinson,   *New Jersey*
Samuel V. Disborough,   *New Jersey*
Albert Baldwin Dod,   *New York*
John R. Livingston, Jr.,   *New York*
James Alfred Pearce,   *Maryland*
Edward Dunlap Smith, *Pennsylvania*,   Valedictory Oration
James William Thompson,   *Virginia*
James Weatherby,   *Pennsylvania*

1823

Joseph W. Smith, *New York*,   Latin Salutatory
John Peter Jackson, *New Jersey*,   English Salutatory

HONORARY ORATIONS

Edward G. Bourke,   *Maryland*
Isaac S Demund,   *Ohio*
James Ewing, Jr., *New Jersey*,   Latin Oration
James Latimer, Jr., *Delaware*,   Greek Oration
John Gibson McCall,   *New Jersey*
Henry McIlvaine,   *New Jersey*
Henry S. Richards, *New Jersey*,   Valedictory Oration
John Slosson,   *New York*

Augustine J Smith,	*Virginia*
Henry Stout,	*Delaware*
Daniel Weisel,	*Maryland*
Nicholas Arrowsmith Wilson,	*New Jersey*

1824

| Bowes Reed Brown *New Jersey*, | Latin Salutatory |
| James Adams, *North Carolina*, | English Salutatory |

HONORARY ORATIONS

George Washington Baker, *New Jersey*,	Greek Oration
Robert Boyd Campfield,	*New Jersey*
David Crawford, *District of Columbia*,	Valedictory Oration
Francis Armstrong Ewing,	*New Jersey*
David Moffat Halliday,	*New Jersey*
Robert W Halsted,	*New Jersey*
Henry Helmuth Krebs,	*Pennsylvania*
George Plum Molleson,	*New Jersey*
John Pearson,	*New York*
Jesse B Pitt,	*New Jersey*
John C. Porter,	*New York*
Richard W Ringgold,	*Maryland*
John Small,	*Maryland*
John Neilson Taylor,	*New Jersey*
James R Wilson,	*New Jersey*

1825

| William Picclees Alrichs, *Delaware*, | Latin Salutatory |
| James Dinsmore Pickands, *Pennsylvania*, | English Salutatory |

HONORARY ORATIONS

Abraham Rezeau Brown,	*New Jersey*
Charles Campbell,	*Virginia*
Frederick Frelinghuysen Cornell, *New Jersey*,	Greek Oration
James I W Davies, *Georgia*,	Valedictory Oration
William Lewis Dayton,	*New Jersey*

Abraham Hagaman,   *New Jersey*
Joseph M Heister,   *Pennsylvania*
Whitefield Nichols,   *New Jersey*
John B. Piessley,   *South Carolina*
Thomas Ross,   *Pennsylvania*
John Vaughan Smith,   *Pennsylvania*
Thomas M Wadsworth,   *North Carolina*
Daniel McCalla Witherspoon,   *Kentucky*
Abraham Oothout Zabriskie,   *New Jersey*

1826

Petei McCall, *New Jersey*,   Latin Salutatory
William Barclay Napton, *New Jersey*,   English Salutatory

HONORARY ORATIONS

Joseph Addison Alexander, *New Jersey*,   Valedictory Oration
William Bainbridge,   *District of Columbia*
Daniel Baikalow,   *New Jersey*
George Washington Bolling,   *Virginia*
David Comfort, Jr.,   *New Jersey*
Joseph D. Condit,   *New Jersey*
Hamilton Claverhouse Graham,   *North Carolina*
Thomas D James,   *New Jersey*
Isaac Jenkins Mikell,   *South Carolina*
John Jacob Ridgway,   *Pennsylvania*
Martyn Tupper,   *Connecticut*
Robert Van Arsdale,   *New Jersey*
James Henry Watkins,   *Maryland*

1827

Joseph C Clarke, *Mississippi*,   Latin Salutatory
James Speer, *New Jersey*,   English Salutatoiy

HONORARY ORATIONS

Edward M Biddle,   *Pennsylvania*
David Nevius Bogart,   *New Jersey*
Jonathan Bailey Condit, *New Jersey*,   Greek Oration

John Z Davenport,   *Virginia*
Tobias Epstein, *Pennsylvania*,   Valedictory Oration
William S. Faitoute,   *New Jersey*
William King McDonald,   *District of Columbia*
Jacob Duché Mitchell,   *Pennsylvania*
George S Pepper,   *Pennsylvania*
James Clemson Watson,   *Pennsylvania*
Benjamin Williamson,   *New Jersey*

1828

Samuel Hubbell, *Connecticut*,   Latin Salutatory
John Oswald Thompson, *Pennsylvania*,   English Salutatory

HONORARY ORATIONS

John G Andrews,   *Mississippi*
Samuel Reading Bertron,   *Pennsylvania*
Edward B Brien,   *Maryland*
Richard B Carmichael, *Maryland*,   Valedictory Oration
William Scudder Cooley,   *New Jersey*
John Strawbridge Corbin,   *Virginia*
William Lygon Corbin,   *Virginia*
George C. Forsyth,   *New Jersey*
Theodore M Hart,   *Pennsylvania*
Samuel Higgins McDonald,   *New Jersey*
Charles Champe Taliaferro,   *Virginia*
Alfred Alexander Woodhull,   *New Jersey*
John Neilson Woodhull,   *New Jersey*

1829

William Pepper, *Pennsylvania*,   Latin Salutatory
Henry N Martin, *Maryland*,   English Salutatory

HONORARY ORATIONS

Richard Ross Crawford,   *District of Columbia*
Festus Hanks,   *Vermont*
George William Leyburn,   *Virginia*
Peter Lott,   *New Jersey*

Archibald Maclean,   *New Jersey*
Stokes L Roberts,   *Pennsylvania*
Benjamin Rush,[1] *Pennsylvania,*   Valedictory Oration
Robert Skinner,   *Maryland*
Jonathan Bayard H. Smith,   *District of Columbia*
Samuel Stanhope Smith,   *Louisiana*
Albert Williams,   *New Jersey*
James Wyckoff,   *New Jersey*

1830

James Cooke Edwards, *New Jersey,*   Latin Salutatory
Harris Lindsay Sproat, *Pennsylvania,*   English Salutatory

HONORARY ORATIONS

De Pui Field,   *New Jersey*
Charles Nicholas Hagner,   *District of Columbia*
John Seely Hart, *Pennsylvania,*   Valedictory Oration
James McDougall,   *New Jersey*
John Plotts,   *New Jersey*
Martin John Ryerson,   *New Jersey*
John Beatty Scudder,   *New Jersey*
William B. Sloan,   *New Jersey*
James Stratton,   *New Jersey*
Thomas E. Van Bibber,   *Maryland*
Hugh Nesbit Wilson,   *New Jersey*

1831

FIRST HONOR[2]

Samuel Galloway, *Pennsylvania,*   English Salutatory
William Bryan Hart,   *Pennsylvania*
James Pollock, *Pennsylvania,*   Greek Oration
George Washington Smythe, *New Jersey,*   Latin Salutatory

---

[1] Mr. Rush being absent on account of illness, the Valedictory oration was delivered by Festus Hanks of Vermont

[2] From *MS Diary of William Elmer*, class of 1832

Second Honor

James Murray Rush, *Pennsylvania*,   Valedictory Oration

Honorary Orations

Samuel Hardenbrook Black,	*New Jersey*
Archibald Alexander Caruthers,	*Virginia*
John Howell Condit,	*New Jersey*
Benjamin Cory,	*New Jersey*
William Henry Drake,	*New York*
Cornelius Henry Edgar,	*New Jersey*
Jared Leigh Elliott,	*District of Columbia*
John Pringle Jones,	*Pennsylvania*
Edward M. Miller,	*New Jersey*
Elihu Pierson,	*New Jersey*
William Townley,	*New Jersey*
Luther Halsey Van Doren,	*New York*

1832[1]

First Honor

George Burrowes, *New Jersey*,   Latin Salutatory

Second Honor

George Dod Armstrong,	*New Jersey*
William Elmer, *New Jersey*,	English Salutatory
Henry D Mandeville, *Pennsylvania*,	Honorary Oration
George Washington Nevitt,	*Mississippi*
Ernst H Ogden,	*New Jersey*

Third Honor

Charles Beatty Green Guild,	*Pennsylvania*
John Steward, *New York*,	Honorary Oration

---

[1] The honors for this year are taken from the *MS Diary of William Elmer*, class of 1832   The outbreak of Asiatic cholera, during the summer of 1832, temporarily closed the College and prevented an elaborate Commence-

John Stryker,   *New Jersey*
Joseph Marsh Taylor,   *New Jersey*

———

John Forsyth, Jr ,[1] *Georgia*,   Valedictory Oration

1833

Martin Ryerson, *New Jersey*,   Latin Salutatory
John Provost, *New Jersey*,   English Salutatory

HONORARY ORATIONS

Charles H Beale,   *Virginia*
John Riggs Crane,   *New Jersey*
Adam Stephen Dandridge,   *Virginia*
Charles Squire Dod,   *New Jersey*
William Dod, *New Jersey*,   Valedictory Oration
David J Halsted,   *New York*
Alexander C. Hart,   *Pennsylvania*
Paul Townsend Jones,   *South Carolina*
David S Kaufman,   *Pennsylvania*
John Leyburn,   *Virginia*
William McCullough,   *Pennsylvania*
Jotham Smith,   *New York*
Spencer S. Sproat,   *Pennsylvania*
Joseph Buck Stratton,   *New Jersey*
Fielding L. Turner,   *Mississippi*
David Van Deren,   *New Jersey*
Joshua Maddox Wallace,   *New Jersey*
Matthias Ward,   *New Jersey*

JUNIOR ORATORS
Cliosophic Society

Parke Godwin,   *New Jersey*
Melancthon Williams Jacobus,   *New Jersey*

ment It is believed there were no Junior Orations. No newspaper accounts
of the proceedings of this Commencement appear

[1] Sixth honor group   *MS Diary of William Elmer*

Elias Jones Richards,   *New York*
John B Taylor,   *New Jersey*

American Whig Society

John T A. Dearing,   *Georgia*
Joseph Fisher Leaming,   *New Jersey*
James J Okill,[1]   *New York*
Nicholas H. Shipley,   *Maryland*

1834

Melancthon Williams Jacobus, *New Jersey*,   Latin Salutatory
Edmund Pendleton, *Virginia*,   English Salutatory

Honorary Orations

Lewis Penn Worthington Balch,   *Maryland*
John Crowell,   *Pennsylvania*
Joseph Austin Davis,   *New Jersey*
John T A. Dearing,   *Georgia*
Parke Godwin,   *New Jersey*
Littleton James Johnson,   *Virginia*
Joseph Fisher Leaming,   *New Jersey*
Henry Van Dyke Nevius,   *District of Columbia*
Richard R. Paulison,   *New Jersey*
Elias Jones Richards,   *New York*
Frederick William Shelton, *New Jersey*,   Valedictory Oration
Nicholas H Shipley,   *Maryland*
Charles S Sibley,   *New Jersey*
George Rice Smith,   *Maryland*
John B Taylor,   *New Jersey*
Daniel Wells,   *New York*
Edward William Whelpley,   *New Jersey*

1835

Levi Janvier, *New Jersey*,   Latin Salutatory
James McClune, *Pennsylvania*,   English Salutatory

---

[1] Of the Freshman class (1836)

Honorary Orations

Richard Maxwell Baker,	*Georgia*
John Barnwell Campbell,	*South Carolina*
James Chestnut,	*South Carolina*
Alexander Hamilton Dodge,	*District of Columbia*
Peter Hamilton,	*New Jersey*
James Giles Hampton,	*New Jersey*
Charles Kisselman Imbrie,	*Pennsylvania*
George Armistead Leakin,	*Maryland*
John Sears McCulloh,	*Maryland*
James Clement Moffat,[1]	*Scotland*
Joseph Owen,	*New York*
William Paterson,	*New Jersey*
John Cunningham Patterson,	*Delaware*
William Post, Jr ,	*New York*
Horace Binney Wallace,	*Pennsylvania*
George Maxwell Wilson,	*Virginia*
William Sidney Wilson, *Maryland*,	Valedictory Oration

Junior Oraiors

Cliosophic Society

Jonathan Pennington Alward,	*New Jersey*
John D. Shelton,	*New York*
John Elliott Thompson,	*Pennsylvania*
Samuel Lawrence Tuttle,	*New Jersey*

American Whig Society

John M Edgar,	*Maryland*
Allan Murray Jerome,	*New York*
John Stevenson Maxwell,	*New York*
James J Okill,	*New York*

---

[1] J C. Moffat delivered the Valedictory oration, *vice* W S Wilson, excused

1836[1]

Benjamin Rice Baird, *Virginia*,	Latin Salutatory
John Miller, *New Jersey*,	English Salutatory
Robert Lenox Maitland,	*New York*
Richard Sears McCulloh,	*Maryland*
Lewis W Williams,	*Pennsylvania*
John Alfred Kanouse,	*New Jersey*

———

John Thomson Mason,[2] *Maryland*,	Valedictory Oration

Junior Orators

Cliosophic Society

Alexander Hamilton Bailey,	*New York*
David Conger,	*New York*
Jehiel Jaggar Post,	*New York*
William C Storrs,	*New York*

American Whig Society

William Churchill Houston Brown,	*New Jersey*
Joshua Hall McIlvaine,	*Delaware*
Alexander Gardiner Mercer,	*Pennsylvania*
John Newland,	*New York*

1837

John Hamilton Townley, *New Jersey*,	Latin Salutatory
John Newland, *New York*,	English Salutatory
Joseph Branch, *North Carolina*,	Greek Oration
Frederick Knighton,	*New Jersey*
Joshua Hall McIlvaine,	*Delaware*

[1] The names for this and succeeding years are arranged in the order of scholarship, from the maximum grade of 100 to that of 90, inclusive   The lists represent each man's average for the whole course of four years, and are taken from the official records in the minutes of the Faculty.

[2] J T Mason stood thirty-eighth in scholarship, with an average of 63 1, and was appointed Valedictorian because of his excellence as an orator

Benjamin Haines Williams,   *New Jersey*
Fenton Mercer Henderson,   *Virginia*
Caleb Smith Green,   *New Jersey*

———

Alexander Gardiner Mercer,[1] *Pennsylvania*,

Valedictory Oration

1838

Daniel Johnson, *North Carolina*,   Latin Salutatory
John Irwin Smith,   *Maryland*
Abner Addison Porter, *Alabama*,   English Salutatory
Lewis Jeffery Williams,   .   *Maryland*
Benjamin Boisseau Vaughan,   *Virginia*
Lawrence O'Brian Branch,   *North Carolina*
William Edward Schenck,   *New Jersey*
Theodore Little,   *New Jersey*
James Madison Allen,   *Virginia*
Samuel G. Williams,   *South Carolina*
Jonathan Cory,   *New Jersey*
William Armstrong Dod,   *New Jersey*
Thomas Colman Montgomery,   *New York*

———

Josiah Willard Gibbs,[2] *Pennsylvania*,   Valedictory Oration

Junior Orators

Cliosophic Society

Henry Mills Fuller,   *Pennsylvania*
William Brutus H. Howard,   *Alabama*

---

[1] The Valedictory oration was delivered by Joseph H Dukes of South Carolina, *vice* A G M⸱⸱⸱r, absent on account of illness (*Princeton Whig*, Sept 29, 1837) Mercer's average was 77 8, that of Dukes, 87 5 *Minutes of the Faculty*, August 14, 1837

[2] In the published list of Commencement orators, which appeared in the *New Jersey State Gazette* of Sept 28, 1838, Lawrence O'B Branch is said to have delivered the English Salutatory, and Abner A Porter the Valedictory

Walter Preston,   *Virginia*
Abner Wentworth Clopton Terry,   *Virginia*

American Whig Society

Neill Smith Graham,   *Alabama*
Henry Kent McCay,   *Pennsylvania*
George H B Matthews,   *Alabama*
Joel Parker,   *New Jersey*

1839

William Miller Reese,[1] *Georgia*,   Latin Salutatory
Alexander M Scudder, *New Jersey*,   English Salutatory
Jesse Edwards,   *New York*
Jacob Belville,   *Pennsylvania*
Stephen H Conger,[2]   *New York*
Mahlon Long,   *Pennsylvania*
Francis Aloysius Baker,   *Maryland*
Henry Augustine Washington,   *Virginia*
George Clinton Bush,   *New York*
James S Colwell,   *Pennsylvania*
Frederick Frelinghuysen Judd,   *New Jersey*
Albert Dabney,   *Virginia*
Theodore M Porter,   *Alabama*

Walter Preston,[3] *Virginia*,   Valedictory Oration

Junior Orators

Cliosophic Society

James Mitchell Cake,   *Virginia*
Thomas Lawrence Jones,   *South Carolina*

oration   The original appointees were frequently excused by the Faculty,
who assigned substitutes, but the honor belongs with the original choice
Gibbs' average was 76 7   *Minutes of the Faculty*, August 13, 1838

[1] Reese was excused from speaking by the Faculty   Scudder then delivered the Latin and Edwards the English Salutatory orations   *Ibid.*

[2] Conger and Long equal, average 95 7   *Ibid*

[3] Preston's average for the four years' course was 71 7   *Ibid*

Daniel Wagener,   *Pennsylvania*
Perry Snowden Warfield,   *Louisiana*

American Whig Society

Henry Martyn Alexander,   *New Jersey*
Ellis B Schnabel,   *Pennsylvania*
Nathaniel G Taylor,   *Tennessee*
Franklin Tilford,   *Kentucky*

1840

Charles John Morris Gwinn, *Maryland,*   Latin Salutatory
Levi Hunt Christian, *New Jersey,*   English Salutatory
Jeremiah De Klyn Lalor,   *New Jersey*
Daniel Wagener,   *Pennsylvania*
John Shaw Pierson,   *New York*
John Whelen Sterling,   *Pennsylvania*
William H Lemoine,   *Virginia*
W. Chauncey Brooks,   *Virginia*
John Jacob Crane,   *Connecticut*
John Stillwell Schanck,   *New Jersey*
Jehu Patterson,   *New Jersey*
Thomas Harvey Rodman,   *New Jersey*
Samuel L Pitcher,   *Virginia*
William Alexander Little,   *Virginia*
James Alexander Darrah,[1]   *Pennsylvania*
Constantine J Menæos,   *Greece*
Anastasius Menæos,   *Greece*

———

John Monroe Banister,[2] *Virginia,*   Valedictory Oration

Junior Orators
Cliosophic Society

Theodore Ledyard Cuyler,   *New York*
Frederick S. Giger,   *Maryland*

[1] Darrah and C. J Menæos equal in scholarship *Minutes of the Faculty,*
August 18, 1840
[2] Banister's average was 82 6   *Ibid*

R. Lawler Smith,   *Mississippi*
Richard Wilde Walker,   *Alabama*

American Whig Society

Joseph Mayo Atkinson,   *Virginia*
John Thompson Nixon,   *New Jersey*
James Webb Rodgers,   *Tennessee*
John McDonald Ross,   *Cherokee Nation*

1841

Amzi Dodd, *New Jersey*,   Latin Salutatory
Thomas Mundell Keerl, *Maryland*,   English Salutatory
Theodore Ledyard Cuyler,   *New York*
John Thomas Duffield,   *Pennsylvania*
Caleb Cook Baldwin, Jr.,   *New Jersey*
George Musgrave Giger,   *Maryland*
John P Dunham,   *New York*
Ludlow Day Potter,   *New Jersey*
James P. Miller,   *New Jersey*
Nathan Merritt Owen,   *New York*
Henry Parkhurst Johnson,   *New Jersey*

Richard Wilde Walker,[1] *Alabama*,   Valedictory Oration

JUNIOR ORATORS

Cliosophic Society

Charles Abert,   *District of Columbia*
James Bowen Everhart,   *Pennsylvania*
James Monroe Murphy,   *South Carolina*
Benjamin Thomas Phillips,   *New York*

American Whig Society

Archibald Woods Paull,   *Virginia*
William Potter Ross,   *Cherokee Nation*

---

[1] Walker's average was 76 9   *Minutes of the Faculty*, August 17, 1841

Thomas Sparrow, Jr ,   *North Carolina*
John S. Telfair,   *North Carolina*

1842

Joseph Jackson Halsey, *New Jersey*,   Latin Salutatory
Stephen G Woodbridge, *New Jersey*,   English Salutatory
Joseph Fithian Garrison,   *New Jersey*
Thomas Ware Cattell,   *New Jersey*
Robert King Stone,   *District of Columbia*
Thomas Nesbit MacCarter,   *New Jersey*
James Bowen Everhart,   *Pennsylvania*
Thomas Sparrow, Jr., *North Carolina*,   Valedictory Oration
Elijah Richardson Craven,   *District of Columbia*

JUNIOR ORATORS

Cliosophic Society

David Terrell Bagley,   *Louisiana*
George Phillips Blevins,   *Alabama*
Oliver Porter Stark,   *New York*
Benjamin Chambers Wickes,   *Maryland*

American Whig Society

Henry N. Beach,   *New Jersey*
James Hazzard Cuthbert,   *South Carolina*
Henry Clay Pindell,   *Kentucky*
Richard Stockton,   *New Jersey*

1843

John Joseph Entwisle, *Maryland*,   Latin Salutatory
Philip Cressman, Jr , *Pennsylvania*,   English Salutatory
Henry Clay Pindell,   *Kentucky*
John J Olcott,   *New York*
Richard P Llewellyn Baber,   *Virginia*
Jonathan Townley Crane,   *New Jersey*
Westcott Wilkin,   *New York*
William Gledhill,   *New Jersey*

Benjamin Chambers Wickes,[1]	*Maryland*
John Pinkerton,	*Pennsylvania*
William Jones Stone, Jr.,	*District of Columbia*
Richard Ignatius Wilson,	*Tennessee*
James Hazzard Cuthbert,	*South Carolina*
Job Symmes Crane,	*New Jersey*

George Phillips Blevins,[2] *Alabama,*   Valedictory Oration

Junior Orators

Cliosophic Society

Alfred Holt Colquitt,	*Georgia*
Green Pulaski Foute,	*Mississippi*
William Pannill, Jr.,	*Virginia*
John H Thomas,	*Maryland*

American Whig Society

Robert Waight Fuller,	*South Carolina*
Samuel P Hill,	*North Carolina*
Hugh Boudinot Johnston,	*North Carolina*
James W. Watson,	*Mississippi*

1844

William Pannill, Jr , *Virginia,*	Latin Salutatory
Benjamin Burton,[3] *Connecticut,*	English Salutatory
Allan Macfarlan,	*Scotland*
Edward Mills Dodd,	*New Jersey*
James Clarke Welling,	*New Jersey*
Joseph Hiester Blackfan,	*New Jersey*
Archibald Alexander Little,	*Virginia*
George Johnson,	*Mississippi*

---

[1] Wickes and Pinkerton equal in scholarship, average 91 6   *Minutes of the Faculty,* August 17, 1843

[2] Mr Blevins' average in scholarship for the full course was 81 8   *Ibid*

[3] According to the New Jersey *State Gazette* (June 28, 1844), Dodd delivered the English Salutatory and Macfarlan the Valedictory   See note 2, p 41

John Owen, Jr.,   *New York*
Henry Reeves,   *New Jersey*
Joseph Woods Pinkerton,   *Pennsylvania*
William Beekman Gulick,   *New Jersey*
Charles Augustus Bennett,   *New Jersey*
Luther Littell,   *New Jersey*

———

Henry Cousins Chambers,[1] *Alabama*,   Valedictory Oration

JUNIOR ORATORS

Cliosophic Society

William Leslie Harris,   *South Carolina*
Charles Godfrey Leland,   *Pennsylvania*
Thomas Murphy,   *New York*
David D Sanderson,   *Alabama*

American Whig Society

A. Hamilton Balentine,   *Pennsylvania*
Albert M. Brown,   *Maryland*
Alexander Reid,   *New York*
Furman Sheppard,   *New Jersey*

1845

Charles Moreau Davis, *New Jersey*,   Latin Salutatory
Thomas Murphy, *New York*,   English Salutatory
Alexander C Taylor,   *New Jersey*
Edward Lewis,   *Ohio*
Alexander John Graham,   *New Jersey*
N Byron Smith,   *New Jersey*
Albert Montgomery Dupuy,   *Virginia*
William Leslie Harris,   *South Carolina*
Silas C. Cook, Jr.,   *Pennsylvania*

---

[1] Henry C Chambers was absent from the latter part of the final Senior examination, on account of severe illness   The average of his previous standing in scholarship was 94 2   *Minutes of the Faculty*, June 7, 1844.

Alexander Reid,	*New York*
Samuel Wills Carey,	*New Jersey*
Robert Allen,	*New Jersey*
James C Beach,	*New York*
Edwin S. Lemoine,	*Virginia*
Walter Mann,	*Iowa*
A. Hamilton Balentine,	*Pennsylvania*
Furman Sheppard, *New Jersey*,	Valedictory Oration

JUNIOR ORATORS

Cliosophic Society

John Alexander Annin,	*New Jersey*
John Fabian Baker,	*Pennsylvania*
Joseph Manning Cleaveland,	*New York*
Allen C Milliken,	*Pennsylvania*

American Whig Society

William Munford Baker,	*Mississippi*
Nathaniel Clark Burt,	*New Jersey*
John Patterson Lundy,	*Pennsylvania*
Henry Sturges,	*Virginia*

1846

Stephen Grover Dodd, *New Jersey*,	Latin Salutatory
William Hampton Babbitt,[1] *New Jersey*,	English Salutatory
Nathaniel Clark Burt, *New Jersey*,	Valedictory Oration
John Fabian Baker,	*Pennsylvania*
Robert F Dennis,	*New Jersey*
John Alexander Annin,	*New Jersey*
Henry Taylor,	*Virginia*
John R. Baltzell,	*Maryland*
William E. T. Griffith,	*Mississippi*
Ashbel Green,	*New Jersey*
Frank Key Dunlop,	*District of Columbia*

---

[1] Babbitt and Burt equal in scholarship, average 98   *Minutes of the Faculty*, May 18, 1846

David Ayres Depue,	*New Jersey*
Gilbert Combs,	*New Jersey*
Levin Thomas Handy Irving,	*Maryland*
William Munford Baker,	*Mississippi*
Thomas Kirkman, Jr ,	*Alabama*
Ambrose Yoemans Moore,	*Michigan*

Junior Orators

Cliosophic Society

William Armstrong Blevins,	*Alabama*
Robert Foster,	*New Jersey*
Charles Howard Key,	*District of Columbia*
George Maxwell Robeson,	*New Jersey*

American Whig Society

William Hepburn Armstrong,	*Pennsylvania*
Hiester Clymer,	*Pennsylvania*
Daniel Elliott,	*Georgia*
William Henry Welsh,	*Pennsylvania*

1847

Henry Rinker, *Pennsylvania*,	Latin Salutatory
Henry Clay Cameron,[1] *Virginia*,	English Salutatory
Beverley Randolph Wellford, Jr , *Virginia*,	Valedictory Oration
John Montgomery Candor,	*Illinois*
Nathan A Cooper Seward,	*New Jersey*
Thaddeus Ainsworth Culbertson,	*Pennsylvania*
Thomas Scott Henderson McCay,	*Mississippi*
John Gosman,	*New York*
David S Garland Cabell,	*District of Columbia*
John Glassell, Jr.,	*Virginia*
Henry Benson Munn,	*New Jersey*
Robert Foster,	*New Jersey*
Montgomery Johns,	*Maryland*

[1] The scholarship of Cameron and Wellford for the whole course was equal, being 98 *Minutes of the Faculty*, May 24, 1847

Junior Orators
Cliosophic Society

William M Gillaspie,	*Mississippi*
Vindex Keirn,	*Mississippi*
Charles Stewart Perkins,	*Mississippi*
James Stevenson,	*Ireland*

American Whig Society

William Cassidy Cattell,	*New Jersey*
Fayette Clapp,	*New York*
James McMullin Crowell,	*Pennsylvania*
Cornelius Williams Tolles,	*New Jersey*

1848

Caspar Wistar Hodge, *New Jersey*,	Latin Salutatory
John Edwards, *New York*,	English Salutatory
Thomas Dobie Davidson,	*Virginia*
William Cassidy Cattell,	*New Jersey*
James McMullin Crowell,	*Pennsylvania*
Charles White,	*Virginia*
Edward Barry Wall, *New York*,	Valedictory Oration
Thomas George Wall,	*New York*
George Reed Morehouse,	*New Jersey*
Henry Cooper Pitney,	*New Jersey*
George Blagden Stone,	*District of Columbia*
John Henderson,[1]	*Virginia*
Arthur Whiteley,	*Delaware*
Cornelius Williams Tolles,	*New Jersey*

Junior Orators
Cliosophic Society

George Hollenback Butler,	*Pennsylvania*
William E Hamilton,	*New Jersey*

[1] Henderson and Whiteley equal, average 90.9　*Minutes of the Faculty*, June 2, 1848

Samuel Robb,   *Pennsylvania*
Marcellus E. Vason,   *Georgia*

American Whig Society

Landon Carter Eliason,   *Virginia*
Edwin Emerson,   *New York*
Thomas Brainerd Harrington,   *Massachusetts*
Richard H. Simms,   *District of Columbia*

1849

William Armstrong Ingham, *Pennsylvania*,   Latin Salutatory
Richard James Gittings,[1] *Maryland*,   English Salutatory
Samuel Robb, *Pennsylvania*,   Valedictory Oration
Basil Lanneau Gildersleeve, *Virginia*,   Belles Lettres Oration
Paul E. Lemoine,   *Virginia*
Charles Newton Campbell, *Virginia*,   Mathematical Oration
Peter Augustus Studdiford, *New Jersey*,   Classical Oration
James Alexander Paige,   *Ohio*
James Henry Leps,   *Virginia*
George Duffield Holmes,   *Tennessee*
James Kendall Lee,   *Virginia*
Theodore Linn Byington,   *New Jersey*
Landon Carter Eliason,   *Virginia*
Edwin Emerson,   *New York*
Marcus Jediah Wallace,   *Tennessee*
Lewis Harvey Wade,   *New Jersey*
Cameron McCaskill, *Alabama*,   Philosophical Oration
Edmund McKnight Tingle,   *Maryland*
Ezra Mundy Hunt,   *New Jersey*
James Wilson Taylor,   *New York*
George Langstaff,   *New Jersey*
Frank Henderson,[2]   *Mississippi*
Bradley Tyler Johnson,   *Maryland*

[1] Gittings and Robb equal in scholarship, average 97 8   *Minutes of the Faculty*, May 21, 1849.

[2] Henderson and Johnson equal, average 90   *Ibid*

Junior Orators

Cliosophic Society

William Elliott Baker,	*Pennsylvania*
Archibald Parritt Cobb,	*New Jersey*
Stephen Lyon Mershon,	*New Jersey*
Charles Sergeant,	*New Jersey*

American Whig Society

Charles D. Bonsall,	*Mississippi*
Samuel Everett Pierce,	*New York*
William Lowndes Wells,	*New York*
Edwin Theodore Williams,	*Georgia*

1850[1]

Archibald Parritt Cobb, *New Jersey*,	Latin Salutatory
William Elliott Baker, *Pennsylvania*,	Valedictory Oration
Lachlan C. Vass, *Virginia*,	English Salutatory
William Nicholls Bolling,[2] *Virginia*,	Scientific Oration
William Henry Canfield, *New Jersey*,	Ethical Oration
John Huger Johns, Jr.,[3] *Virginia*,	Honorary Oration
Samuel Everett Pierce, *New York*,	Belles Lettres Oration
Reuel Stewart, *New Jersey*,	Mathematical Oration
Alfred H Barber,	*New Jersey*
Robert Piper Bolling,	*Virginia*
John Wiggins Simonton,	*Pennsylvania*
Lewis Stovel,	*Pennsylvania*
Isaac Amada Cornelison,	*Pennsylvania*
Thomas Anderson,[4]	*New Jersey*
George T Sergeant,	*New Jersey*

[1] Forty-one per cent of the entire class attained an average in scholarship of 90 or above

[2] Bolling and Canfield equal in scholarship, average 97 7   *Minutes of the Faculty*, May 20, 1850.

[3] Johns, Pierce, and Stewart equal, average 96 2   *Ibid.*

[4] Anderson and Sergeant equal, average 93 7   *Ibid*

Daniel Warfield, Jr.,	*Maryland*
Abraham Halsey,	*New Jersey*
Joseph Bardwell,	*Mississippi*
Stephen Lyon Mershon,	*New Jersey*
Lemuel Cobb Howell,	*New Jersey*
William F. Mellon,[1]	*Mississippi*
John Thomas Stockett,	*Maryland*
Charles Sergeant,	*New Jersey*
Edwin Theodore Williams,	*Georgia*
John Taylor Coit,	*South Carolina*
Alexander Miller Woods,	*Pennsylvania*
John A. Marshall,[2]	*Pennsylvania*
Abraham Voorhees,	*New Jersey*
John Eyre Shaw,	*Pennsylvania*
Aldus J Neff,	*Pennsylvania*
William Austin Seay, *Virginia*,	Honorary Oration
John Leander McMillan,	*Mississippi*
James Barbour Grant,	*Maryland*

Junior Orators

Cliosophic Society

Daniel Gould Fowle,	*North Carolina*
William Butler Guild, Jr.,	*New Jersey*
James L McLean,	*New Jersey*
John Benjamin E. Williams,	*North Carolina*

American Whig Society

Barnes Compton,	*Maryland*
Henry Van Dyke Johns, Jr ,	*Maryland*
Frederick Augustus Metcalfe,	*Mississippi*
Jeremiah Howard Nixon,	*New Jersey*

---

[1] Mellon and Stockett equal, average 92 4　*Minutes of the Faculty*, May 20, 1850

[2] Marshall and Voorhees equal, average 90 8　*Ibid*

1851

Edwin Rea Bower, *Pennsylvania*,	Latin Salutatory
Samuel Thomas Thompson, *Pennsylvania*,	English Salutatory
Jeremiah Howard Nixon, *New Jersey*,	Valedictory Oration
George Lewis Crawford, *Pennsylvania*,	Mathematical Oration
George Johnson,	*Maryland*
William Henry Baltzell,	*Maryland*
Peyton Randolph Harrison,	*Virginia*
Archibald Stirling, Jr.,[1]	*Maryland*
William Carter Williams,	*Virginia*
Benjamin Franklin Shreve,	*New Jersey*
Albert T Rhodes,	*Maryland*
David M Cochran,	*Pennsylvania*
Henry G Hall, *Texas*,	Physical Oration
Alexander Hamilton Phillips, Jr.,	*Texas*
Daniel Gould Fowle,	*North Carolina*
William Stevenson Walker,	*Maryland*
Archibald George,[2]	*Maryland*
Henry Van Dyke Johns, Jr ,	*Maryland*
Caleb Davis Shreve,	*New Jersey*
Frederick Augustus Metcalfe,	*Mississippi*
Fullerton Reck Harbaugh,	*Maryland*
William R Friend,	*Alabama*
Lewis Depui Vail,	*Pennsylvania*

JUNIOR ORATORS

Cliosophic Society

Charles Colcock Jones, Jr.,	*Georgia*
James B McRae,	*Mississippi*
Alexander T Niven,	*New York*
William Vance Thompson,	*Tennessee*

[1] Stirling and Williams equal in scholarship, average 96 2   *Minutes of the Faculty*, May 19, 1851

[2] George and Johns equal, average 92 8   *Ibid*

American Whig Society

William J Eckford,	*Mississippi*
James Taylor Jones,	*Alabama*
Austin D Moore,	*Pennsylvania*
Isaac Norton Rendall,	*New York*

1852

Elkanah Dare Mackey, *Pennsylvania*,	Latin Salutatory
William Jay Magie, *New Jersey*,	Valedictory Oration
Solomon S. Schultz, *Pennsylvania*,	English Salutatory
Joseph Addison Freeman, *New Jersey*,	Mathematical Oration
Horace Graham Hinsdale,	*New York*
Gilbert Tennent Woodhull,	*New Jersey*
Alfred Yeomans, *Pennsylvania*,	Fine Arts Oration
Isaac Norton Rendall,	*New York*
Amzi Lewis Armstrong,[1]	*New York*
Sidney Gibbs Law,	*North Carolina*
James Woods, Jr ,	*Tennessee*
Lorenzo Westcott,	*New Jersey*
Joseph Fowler Jennison,	*Pennsylvania*
James Hervey Studdiford,	*New Jersey*
William Vance Thompson,	*Tennessee*
John Van Pelt,	*New Jersey*
Austin D Moore,	*Pennsylvania*
Charles Colcock Jones, Jr ,	*Georgia*
Douglass Patterson,	*Pennsylvania*
Alexander T Niven,	*New York*
Samuel Hirsch,	*Germany*
Louis A Barr,	*Maryland*
Elias Nettleton Crane,	*New York*
William Corbit Spruance,	*Delaware*
De Witt Clinton Mather,	*New York*
Andrew Jackson Dull,[2]	*Pennsylvania*

[1] Armstrong and Law equal in scholarship, average 97 4　　*Minutes of the Faculty*, May 21, 1852

[2] Dull and Phelps equal in scholarship, average 92 1　　*Ibid*

Charles Edward Phelps,	*Maryland*
James Carnahan McDonald,	*New Jersey*
George Morrison,	*Maryland*
Alexander Shaw Field,	*Texas*

JUNIOR ORATORS

Cliosophic Society

William Burwell Fraley,	*Georgia*
Joseph Jones,	*Georgia*
Daniel Du Bois Sahler,	*New York*
John Craig Schenck,	*New Jersey*

American Whig Society

William Jefferson Buchanan,	*Maryland*
Charles Russell Clarke,	*New York*
William Alexander Henry,	*District of Columbia*
Calvin Douglass Mehaffey,	*Pennsylvania*

1853

John Ledyard Hodge, *Louisiana,*	Latin Salutatory
Jeremiah Smith Gordon, *Pennsylvania,*	English Salutatory
Charles Russell Clarke, *New York,*	
	Belles Lettres and Valedictory Oration
Edward W Condict, *New Jersey,*	Classical Oration
Henry Boyd McKeen,	*Pennsylvania*
Christian Henry Scharff,	*New Jersey*
William Erskine Skinner,	*Scotland*
John Craig Schenck,	*New Jersey*
Joseph Jones,	*Georgia*
Thomas Mifflin Hall,	*New Jersey*
William Bennett Scarborough,	*New Jersey*
John Dickson,	*Pennsylvania*
Silas Merchant, Jr,	*New Jersey*
Stewart Brown,	*Maryland*
Oliver S. Belden,	*New Jersey*
Samuel Alexander McElhinny,	*Pennsylvania*

Joseph Alward,	*New Jersey*
Abram Hoogland La Monte,[1]	*New York*
George Pierson, *New Jersey*,	Mathematical Oration
John Torrey, Jr.,	*New Jersey*
Edward H Sholl,	*New York*
Charles Thomas Haley,	*New York*
James Buchanan Henry,	*Pennsylvania*
Daniel Du Bois Sahler,	*New York*

JUNIOR ORATORS

Cliosophic Society

Robert Burton Anderson,	*North Carolina*
Lewis Carter Baker,	*New Jersey*
Addison Waddell Woodhull,	*New Jersey*
Joseph Campbell Wyckoff,	*New Jersey*

American Whig Society

Charles Boyd,	*New York*
James Thomas Coleman,	*Mississippi*
William Henry Goldthwaite,	*Alabama*
Clinton C Gurnee, Jr ,	*New York*

1854

Lewis Carter Baker, *New Jersey*,	Latin Salutatory
William Thomas Morrison, *New York*,	English Salutatory
Richard Marvin Strong, *New York*,	Mathematical Oration
Henry Carrington Alexander, *New York*,	Belles Lettres Oration
Samuel Southard Force,	*District of Columbia*
Frank Chandler,	*New Jersey*
James McDougall,	*New York*
Addison Waddell Woodhull,	*New Jersey*
Sanford Huntington Smith,	*New Jersey*
William Campbell Soutter,	*Pennsylvania*
Samuel Randolph Forman,	*New Jersey*
Thaddeus Burr Wakeman, *New York*,	Ethical Oration

[1] La Monte and Pierson equal in scholarship, average 93 7   *Minutes of the Faculty*, May 23, 1853

Henry Addison Harlow,	*New York*
Charles Boyd, *New York*,	Valedictory Oration
William House,	*New York*
Matthew Wilden Edmonds,[1]	*New Jersey*
Robert Hamill Nassau,	*New Jersey*
Archibald Alexander Edward Taylor,	*Ohio*
John Darroch,[2]	*North Carolina*
John Prentiss Poe,	*Maryland*
Benjamin Smith Condit,	*New Jersey*
John Speed Hanan,	*Maryland*
Edward Dickson Pierson,	*New Jersey*
William Morgan Wells,[3]	*Pennsylvania*
Joseph Campbell Wyckoff,	*New Jersey*
Calvin Wadhams,	*Pennsylvania*
Robert Gamble,	*Pennsylvania*
Israel Crane,	*New Jersey*
Benjamin Lightner Hewitt,	*Pennsylvania*
Edward Thomas Green,	*New Jersey*
Sandford Reynolds Knapp,	*New York*
Philip Scott Caffrey,	*New Jersey*
William Hollister,	*North Carolina*

JUNIOR ORATORS

Cliosophic Society

Henry Miller Cooper,	*Alabama*
John Martin Henderson,	*New Jersey*
James Pumpelly Lovejoy,	*New York*
John Randolph Malloy,	*South Carolina*

American Whig Society

John Ebenezer Annan,	*Pennsylvania*
Henry Martyn Drewry,	*Virginia*
Henry Flavel Lee,	*New York*
William Cooper Inglis,	*South Carolina*

[1] Edmonds and Nassau equal, average 94 4   *Minutes of the Faculty,* May 20, 1854

[2] Darroch and Poe equal, average 93 8   *Ibid*

[3] Wells and Wyckoff equal, average 91 9   *Ibid*

1855

Theodore McGowan, *Pennsylvania*,	Latin Salutatory
William Collins Handy, *Maryland*,	English Salutatory
John Ebenezer Annan, *Pennsylvania*,	Valedictory Oration
William Alexander Fisher,	*Maryland*
George Gibson Carey, *Maryland*,	Classical Oration
John Campbell Boyd,	*New York*
George Phillips Lockwood,	*New York*
Robert Hayne Andrews,	*Virginia*
Henry Flavel Lee,	*New York*
Randolph Augustus Renz,	*Iowa*
Charles Evert Hedges,[1]	*New Jersey*
Joseph Smith Ludlam, *New York*,	Philosophical Oration
Henry Clay Greenewalt,	*Pennsylvania*
Floyd Augustus Crane,	*New York*
Joseph Wilberforce Martin,	*Arkansas*
William McElwee,	*Pennsylvania*
Henry Sanford Gansevoort,	*New York*
David Radnor Coover,[2]	*Pennsylvania*
Frederick Cox Roberts,	*North Carolina*

Junior Orators

Cliosophic Society

Joseph Tuthill Duryea,	*New York*
George Anderson Mercer,	*Georgia*
Hersey Baylies Parker,	*North Carolina*
Samuel Miller Studdiford,	*New Jersey*

American Whig Society

David Owen Davies,	*Missouri*
James Turner Leftwich,	*Virginia*
William Christie Stitt,	*Pennsylvania*
Pere Lethbury Wickes,	*Maryland*

[1] Hedges and Ludlam equal, average 94 *Minutes of the Faculty*, May 18-19, 1855

[2] Coover and Roberts equal, average 90.2 *Ibid*

1856

John Peter Jackson, Jr., *New Jersey*,	Latin Salutatory
Morris Crater Sutphen, *New Jersey*,	English Salutatory
Joseph Tuthill Duryea, *New York*,	Valedictory Oration
Robert Strong, *New York*,	Scientific Oration
George Henry Burroughs,[1] *New Jersey*,	Philosophical Oration
Frederick Voorhees, *New Jersey*,	Mathematical Oration
Thomas Tabb, *Virginia*,	Metaphysical Oration
David Magie, Jr.,	*New Jersey*
Samuel Southard Halsey,	*New Jersey*
Samuel Claggett Chew, *Maryland*,	Classical Oration
John Stevens Stewart,	*Pennsylvania*
Oscar Henry Young,	*New York*
Andrew Patterson Linn Cochran,	*Pennsylvania*
Benjamin Smith Everitt,	*New York*
John Lowrey,[2]	*New Jersey*
George Anderson Mercer,	*Georgia*
James Houston Eccleston,	*Maryland*
James William Bryant,	*Alabama*
Edward Overton, Jr ,	*Pennsylvania*
Robert Stoutenberg Feagles,	*New York*
Joseph Hodgson, Jr ,	*Virginia*
Samuel Miller Studdiford,	*New Jersey*
Robert Proctor,	*New York*
John Lambert Cadwalader,	*New Jersey*
William Henry Woodward,	*Pennsylvania*
William Jackson Wood,	*New Jersey*
James William Coleman,	*New York*
Hamlin Beattie,	*South Carolina*
Jeremiah Cleveland,	*South Carolina*
Henry Harrison Woolsey,	*New Jersey*
John Crater Sutphen,	*New Jersey*
Hersey Baylies Parker,	*North Carolina*

[1] Burroughs and Voorhees equal in scholarship, average 97 9   *Minutes of the Faculty*, May 17, 1856

[2] Lowrey and Mercer equal, average 95.2.   *Ibid.*

Edward Payson Wood,   *Pennsylvania*
Alfred Alexander Woodhull,   *New Jersey*
Asa Whitehead, Jr ,   *New Jersey*

JUNIOR ORATORS

Cliosophic Society

Lyell Thomson Adams,   *New York*
Calvin Morgan Christy,   *Missouri*
Charles Clement, Jr ,   *Louisiana*
William H. Simmons,   *Mississippi*

American Whig Society

James Addison Henry,   *New Jersey*
Charles Henry Luzenberg,   *Louisiana*
James Steenson Mayne,   *Ireland*
James Douglass Vertner,   *Mississippi*

1857

Robert Means Fuller, *South Carolina*,   Latin Salutatory
John McKelway, Jr , *New Jersey*,   English Salutatory
Joseph Smith Van Dyke, *New Jersey*,   Philosophical Oration
James William Abert Wright, *Mississippi*,   Valedictory Oration
Daniel Seely Gregory, *New York*,   Belles Lettres Oration
Gustave Wilhelm Mayer,   *New Jersey*
Isaac Alstyne Blauvelt,   *New Jersey*
Martin Havens,   *New Jersey*
Wallace De Witt,   *Pennsylvania*
David Henry Mitchell,   *Wisconsin*
John Backer Kugler,   *New Jersey*
Samuel Bayard Dod,   *New Jersey*
James Steenson Mayne,   *Ireland*
Charles Carroll Kibbee,   *New York*
Thomas Ryerson Haines,   *New Jersey*
Henry Pawlington Ross,   *Pennsylvania*
John Stottoff Beekman,   *New Jersey*

Junior Orators

Clsosophic Society

Henry Anson Buttz,	*Pennsylvania*
William Lewis Dayton, Jr ,	*New Jersey*
Charles Stratton Howell,	*New Jersey*
Robert Chadwick Hutchings,	*New York*

American Whig Society

John Van Lear Findlay,	*Maryland*
Morris Hancock Stratton,	*New Jersey*
Cortlandt Van Rensselaer, Jr ,	*New Jersey*
Francis Gregory Wood,	*New York*

1858

John Howard Wurts, *New Jersey*,	Latin Salutatory
McHenry Howard,[1] *Maryland*,	English Salutatory
Franklin Fisk Westcott, *New Jersey*,	Valedictory Oration
John Wherry, *Pennsylvania*,	Philosophical Oration
Morris Hancock Stratton, *New Jersey*,	Belles Lettres Oration
Jacob Scudder Galloway, *New Jersey*,	Philosophical Oration
George McCulloch McGill,[2] *New Jersey*,	Poem
Gershom Hatton Nimmo,	*New York*
William Lewis Dayton, Jr.,	*New Jersey*
Joseph Lindsey Shellabarger,	*Pennsylvania*
Samuel Lewis Phillips,	*District of Columbia*
John McCleery,	*Pennsylvania*
James Richards,	*New York*
Charles Edward Hart,	*New Jersey*
Sterling M. Galt,	*Maryland*
Josiah Simpson Studdiford,	*New Jersey*
Francis Gregory Wood,	*New York*
Andrew Todd McKinney,	*Louisiana*

[1] Howard and Westcott equal in scholarship, average 98 2   *Minutes of the Faculty*, May 24, 1858

[2] McGill and Nimmo equal, average 96 4   *Ibid*

Ellis Plumer Cayce,   *Missouri*
Jeremiah Cooke,[1]   *Pennsylvania*
Matthew Newkirk, Jr ,   *Pennsylvania*
Cortlandt Van Rensselaer, Jr ,   *New Jersey*
Henry Anson Buttz,   *Pennsylvania*
Francis Marion Wood,   *New Jersey*
Joel Campbell,[2]   *New Jersey*
David Rankin Love,   *Pennsylvania*
Job Davidson Randolph,   *Pennsylvania*
William Samuel Shields,   *Tennessee*

Junior Orators

Cliosophic Society

William David Lumpkin,   *Tennessee*
Joseph Haswell Robinson,   *New York*
Henry Everett Russell,   *New York*
Frederick Stump,   *Maryland*

American Whig Society

Thomas Goldthwaite,   *Alabama*
Francis Blanchard Hodge,   *New Jersey*
Telfair Hodgson,   *Virginia*
William Potts Lloyd,   *New Jersey*

1859

Alfred Hosea Kellogg, *Pennsylvania*,   Latin Salutatory
Samuel Richards Colwell,[3] *Pennsylvania*, English Salutatory
Henry Everett Russell, *New York*,   Valedictory Oration
George Washington Ketcham, *New Jersey*,

                                             Philosophical Oration
George Gray,   *Delaware*

---

[1] Cook and Newkirk equal, average 92.1. *Minutes of the Faculty*, May 24, 1858

[2] Campbell and Love equal, average 91 3   *Ibid*

[3] Colwell and Russell equal in scholarship, average 97 1.   *Ibid*, May 21-23, 1859

William Bull Wright,	*New York*
Anderson Lalor Brearley,	*New Jersey*
William Alfred McAtee,	*Maryland*
James Craig,[1]	*Florida*
Fergus Lafayette Kenyon,	*Connecticut*
Joseph Haswell Robinson,	*New York*
William Potts Lloyd,	*New Jersey*
James Buyers Kennedy,	*Pennsylvania*
David Magie, Jr.,	*New York*
Frederick Stump,	*Maryland*
Robert Aaron Condit,[2]	*New York*
Charles Barrett Morris,	*New Jersey*
John Witten Frierson,	*Louisiana*
Edgar Holden, *New Jersey*,	Poem
Ira Percy Clark,	*New York*
Grant Wiedman,	*Pennsylvania*
Julian Darragh Janvier,	*Delaware*

Junior Orators

Cliosophic Society

Samuel Jefferson Humphries,	*Mississippi*
S. Stanhope Orris,	*Pennsylvania*
Ephraim Baynard Seabrook,	*South Carolina*
Philip Livingston Van Rensselaer,	*New Jersey*

American Whig Society

John S Condit,	*New Jersey*
William Crawford Harris,	*Georgia*
John Henry Scofield,	*New York*
William Henry Wright,	*New York*

[1] Craig and Kenyon equal, average 95 2   *Minutes of the Faculty*, May 21–23, 1859

[2] Condit and Morris equal, average 92 5   *Ibid*

1860

William Gildersleeve Upson, *New York*,	Latin Salutatory
James Alfred Pearce, Jr., *Maryland*,	Valedictory Oration
Walter Lowrie Rankin, *New Jersey*,	English Salutatory
George Kerper Bechtel,[1] *New Jersey*,	Chemical Oration
Samuel McCuen Wherry, *Pennsylvania*,	Physical Oration
Montgomery Rogers Hooper, *New Jersey*,	
	Philosophical Oration
Edmund Drake Halsey, *New Jersey*,	Philosophical Oration
William Budd Bodine,	*New Jersey*
Joseph Lamb Bodine,	*New Jersey*
John Selby Frame,	*Illinois*
James Morgan Hart,	*Pennsylvania*
George Murray Gill, Jr .	*Maryland*
Theron Brittain,	*Pennsylvania*
Charles Ewing Green. *New Jersey*,	Classical Oration
William Robert McCay,	*Georgia*
James Waddell Alexander, Jr ,	*New York*
Charles Treat Berry,	*New Jersey*
Calvin De Witt,[2]	*Pennsylvania*
Edward Waterman Evans,	*New Jersey*
William Henry Ford,	*Pennsylvania*
John Henry Scofield,	*New York*
Henry Goldthwaite,	*Alabama*
Daniel Henry Smith,	*New York*
John Lindsay Withrow,	*Pennsylvania*
Frederic Seip,	*Louisiana*
James Suydam Knox,	*New York*
Daniel McLean Shaw,	*New Jersey*
Charles Nicholas Chevrier,	*New Jersey*
Eben Jackson Dickey Cross,	*Maryland*
Samuel King Dennis,	*Maryland*

[1] Bechtel and Wherry equal in scholarship, average 97 9 *Minutes of the Faculty*, May 19–21, 1860

[2] De Witt and Evans equal, average 93 6 *Ibid*

Junior Orators
Cliosophic Society

Charles Beasten, Jr.,	*Delaware*
David Ruddach Frazer,	*Maryland*
James Meeker Ludlow,	*New Jersey*
Edward Seymour Wilde,	*New Jersey*

American Whig Society

Andrew Anderson,	*Florida*
John De Witt,	*Pennsylvania*
Charles Dorr Kellogg,	*New York*
Samuel Thomas Roman,	*Maryland*

1861

John Runkle Emery,[1] *New Jersey*,	Latin Salutatory
John A Winebrener, *Pennsylvania*,	Greek Salutatory
Edward Griffin Read, *New Jersey*,	English Salutatory
Thomson McGowan, *Pennsylvania*,	Valedictory Oration
Charles Dorr Kellogg, *New York*,	Belles Lettres Oration
Alfred Brittin Baker, *Illinois*,	Philosophical Oration
David Judson Atwater, *New Jersey*,	Classical Oration
Charles Kellogg Backus,	*New York*
Charles Young,	*New Jersey*
William John Phillips Morrison,	*India*
William Sutphen Combs,	*New Jersey*
Auguste Armagnac,	*Hayti*
Samuel S. Mitchell,	*Wisconsin*
George Vansyckel Forman,	*New Jersey*
William Elmer, Jr ,[2]	*New Jersey*
James Scrimgeour Wylie, Jr , *New York*,	Poem
George Grantham Smith,	*Pennsylvania*
Jonas Parker Varnum,	*New Hampshire*

[1] Emery and Winebrener equal in scholarship, average 99   *Minutes of the Faculty*, May 18–20, 1861

[2] Elmer and Wylie equal, average 93 9   *Ibid*

Charles Beasten, Jr ,[2]   *Delaware*
Winfield Scott Purviance,   *Pennsylvania*
James Meeker Ludlow,   *New Jersey*
William Augustus Rafferty,   *New Jersey*
Edward Harrison Camp,   *New Jersey*
William Edgar Honeyman,[2]   *New Jersey*
Nehemiah Perry, Jr.,   *New Jersey*
Samuel Read Comfort,   *Virginia*
Henry Fuller,   *New Jersey*
Daniel Deruelle,   *New York*
Leroy Hammond Anderson,   *New Jersey*

JUNIOR ORATORS

Cliosophic Society

William Baldwin,   *Illinois*
John Cochran,   *New Jersey*
Augustus Macdonald,   *New Jersey*
James Wyckoff,   *New Jersey*

American Whig Society

James Comfort,   *Virginia*
Daniel Henderson,   *Pennsylvania*
Benjamin S. Morehouse,   *New Jersey*
Charles William Nassau, Jr.,   *New Jersey*

1862

William D Mershon, *New Jersey*,   Latin Salutatory
Lewis Ward Mudge, *New York*,   Valedictory Oration
Charles Edward Webster, *Pennsylvania*, English Salutatory
William Alexander Holliday, *Indiana*, Philosophical Oration
Walter Butler,   *Illinois*
Henry Young,   *New Jersey*

----

[1] Beasten and Purviance equal, average 92 7   *Minutes of the Faculty,* May 18–20, 1861

[2] Honeyman and Perry equal, average 92 4   *Ibid.*

Joseph Lewis Munn,	*New Jersey*
Edward Read Burkhalter,[1] *New York,*	Metaphysical Oration
James Comfort,	*Virginia*
Henry Seymour Butler,	*New York*
James Johnson Coale,	*Maryland*
Frederic Eichelberger Shearer,	*Pennsylvania*
Edward Sanford Atwater,	*New Jersey*
Thomas Edward Converse,[2]	*Pennsylvania*
Charles Hodge Dod, *New Jersey,*	Belles Lettres Oration
Samuel Hayes Pennington, Jr.,	*New Jersey*
Henry Rankin Freeland,	*New York*
Charles Ellis Young,	*New Jersey*
Charles Dillard Roberts,	*Virginia*
John Giffen,	*Illinois*
Charles William Remington,	*New York*
Isaac Dunton,	*Pennsylvania*
Edward Payson Brewster,	*New Jersey*
Edward Rogers Post,	*New York*

S. Stanhope Orris,[3] *Pennsylvania,*	Classical Oration

Junior Orators

Cliosophic Society

Rensselaer Williams Dayton,	*New Jersey*
James Shepard Dennis,	*New Jersey*
Samuel Augustus Hayt, Jr,	*New York*
Huntington Wolcott Jackson,	*New Jersey*

[1] Burkhalter and Comfort equal in scholarship, average 97 2 *Minutes of the Faculty,* May 16, 1862

[2] Converse and Dod equal, average 94.8. *Ibid*

[3] The following minute appears in regard to S S Orris " Having *of their own motion* determined not to examine Mr Orris with his class, the Faculty have not assigned him his relative position, but have given him the oration to which they judged him to be entitled " (*Ibid*) Mr Orris's standing at the semi-annual examination of December 9–16, 1861, was 97 4

American Whig Society

Daniel Requa Foster,	*New York*
William Preston Smalley,	*New Jersey*
Abraham H Strickler,	*Pennsylvania*
Samuel Smith Stryker, Jr ,	*New Jersey*

1863

Jasper Scudder McIlvaine, *New Jersey*,	Latin Salutatory
Theodore Alling Baldwin,[1] *New Jersey*,	English Salutatory
George William Sheldon, *New Jersey*,	Valedictory Oration
George Boardman Young, *New Jersey*,	Philosophical Oration
James Francis Clark,[2] *Pennsylvania*,	Belles Lettres Oration
Charles Henry Potter, *New Jersey*,	Geological Oration
John Newton Freeman, *New Jersey*,	Physical Oration
William Henry Littell,	*Pennsylvania*
Walter Smith Nichols,	*New Jersey*
Robert Raikes Westcott,	*New Jersey*
Matthew Bonsall Lowrie,	*Pennsylvania*
James Brinckerhoff Vredenburgh,	*New Jersey*
Francis Dubois, Jr.,	*New York*
Peter Zahner,	*Ohio*
Samuel Baird Huey,	*Pennsylvania*
Isaac Fisher Sutphen,	*New Jersey*
Thomas Hanlon,	*New Jersey*
Peter Berrien Pumyea,	*New Jersey*
Henry Rodney Hall,	*Delaware*
Henry Ulyate Swinnerton,	*New Jersey*
Francis Barber Chetwood, Jr.,	*New Jersey*
Daniel Requa Foster,	*New York*
Richard Kelso Cross,	*Maryland*
Rensselaer Williams Dayton,	*New Jersey*
Charles Elvin Hendrickson,	*New Jersey*
Benjamin Thompson,	*Iowa*

---

[1] Baldwin and Sheldon equal in scholarship, average 98 8 *Minutes of the Faculty*, May 18, 1863

[2] Clark and Potter equal, average 96 6 *Ibid*

Junior Orators

Cliosophic Society

Theodore Frederic Sanxay,	*Ohio*
Henry Isaac Sheldon,	*New Jersey*
Seargent Prentiss Stearns,	*New Jersey*
Harvey Converse Warren,	*Pennsylvania*

American Whig Society

Valentine Hummel Berghaus,	*Pennsylvania*
Henry Augustus Boardman, Jr.,	*Pennsylvania*
Samuel Milspaugh Boyd,	*Pennsylvania*
Charles Henry Mathews,	*Pennsylvania*

1864

Edward Denison Ledyard, Jr , *Pennsylvania,*	
	Valedictory Oration
Wilberforce Freeman, *New Jersey,*	Latin Salutatory
William Stewart Cross Webster, *Pennsylvania,*	
	English Salutatory
Henry Isaac Sheldon, *New Jersey,*	Philosophical Oration
William Warren Curtiss, *New York,*	Poem
Samuel Miller Gardner,[1] *New York,*	Philosophical Oration
Richard Stockton Hunter, *Pennsylvania,*	Belles Lettres Oration
James Van Alen Butler,	*Illinois*
Alexander Fullerton, Jr ,	*Pennsylvania*
Benjamin Cory Meeker,	*New Jersey*
Seargent Prentiss Stearns,	*New Jersey*
James Leslie Lupton,	*New Jersey*
Leon Dalsheimer,	*Maryland*
Samuel Milspaugh Boyd,	*Pennsylvania*
Henry Augustus Boardman, Jr ,	*Pennsylvania*
Martin Luther Liggett,	*Pennsylvania*
Edmund Canfield,	*New Jersey*

[1] Gardner and Hunter equal in scholarship, average 97 9 *Minutes of the Faculty,* May 20, 1864

Harvey Converse Warren,   *Pennsylvania*
Thomas Frederick Crane,[1]   *New Jersey*
Galen Wilkins Seiler,   *Pennsylvania*

JUNIOR ORATORS
Cliosophic Society

Joseph Cross, Jr ,   *New Jersey*
Daniel Neil Grummon,   *New Jersey*
Theodore Whitefield Hunt,   *New Jersey*
James Newbold Stratton,   *New Jersey*

American Whig Society

William Stone Abert,   *District of Columbia*
Samuel Baker,   *West Virginia*
Charles Henry McClellan,   *West Virginia*
Robert Sloss,   *New York*

1865

Theodore Whitefield Hunt, *New Jersey*,   Latin Salutatory
Daniel Neil Grummon, *New Jersey*,   Valedictory Oration
Archibald MacMartin,[2] *New York*,   Mathematical Oration
Randolph Stephen Roache, *Indiana*,   English Salutatory
Nicholas Conover Jobs English, *New Jersey*,
                                               Philosophical Oration
Joseph Milton Greene, *New York*,   Philosophical Oration
Edward Payson Rankin, *New Jersey*,   Philosophical Oration
Francis Kitchell Howell, *New Jersey*,   Metaphysical Oration
William Evans Guy, *Ohio*,   Belles Lettres Oration
Joseph Pope Pennington, *New Jersey*,   Physical Oration
William Henry Logan,   *Pennsylvania*
Oscar Keen,[3] *New Jersey*,   Classical Oration

---

[1] Crane and Seiler equal in scholarship, average 90 4   *Minutes of the Faculty*, May 20, 1864

[2] MacMartin and Roache equal, average 97 9   *Ibid*, May 20, 1865

[3] Keen and Sloss equal, average 94 9.   *Ibid*.

Robert Sloss, *New York*,	Belles Lettres Oration
Joseph Cross, Jr ,	*New Jersey*
Augustine Breese,[1]	*Illinois*
Samuel Winchester Reeves	*New Jersey*
Matthew Henry Calkins,	*New York*
Thomas John Chew,[2]	*Maryland*
Charles Freeman Richardson,	*New Jersey*
John Samuel Jessup,[3]	*New Jersey*
George Washington Neal,	*New York*
James Robbins Schanck,	*New Jersey*
James Booth Converse,	*Pennsylvania*
John Upshur Dennis,[4]	*Maryland*
William Francis Shelley,	*Iowa*
Edward Riggs,	*Turkey*
William Miller Kisselman Imbrie, *New Jersey*,	Poem
Edward Houston Scott,	*India*
Samuel Smith Wallen,	*New Jersey*
John Carrington,	*California*
William Jesse Grim,	*Pennsylvania*
Alfred B Dayton,	*New Jersey*
William Jones Boone,	*New York*
Henry Sleigel Myers,[5]	*Pennsylvania*
George Lindenberger Van Bibber,	*Maryland*
William Henry Vail,	*New Jersey*

JUNIOR ORATORS

Cliosophic Society

John Mather Allis,	*New York*
Austin B Blair,	*New Jersey*
John A Cobb,	*New Jersey*
David Brainerd Hunt,	*New Jersey*

[1] Breese and Reeves equal in scholarship, average 94 7   *Minutes of the Faculty*, May 20, 1865

[2] Chew and Richardson equal, average 93 7   *Ibid*

[3] Jessup, Neal, and Schanck equal, average 93 6   *Ibid*

[4] Dennis and Shelley equal, average 92 8   *Ibid*

[5] Myers and Van Bibber equal, average 90 5   *Ibid*

American Whig Society

Otto Bergner,	*California*
Henry Melville Gurley.	*District of Columbia*
John Hall McIlvaine,	*New Jersey*
Miles Wilbur Tate,	*Pennsylvania*

Junior Orator Medalists [1]

Otto Bergner,	First Medal
Henry Melville Gurley,	Second Medal
David Brainerd Hunt,	Third Medal
Miles Wilbur Tate,	Fourth Medal

1866 [2]

John K. Cowen, *Ohio*,	Latin Salutatory
Otto Bergner,[3] *California*,	Valedictory Oration
John Saxton Sherrill, *New York*,	English Salutatory
Robert Harbison, *Connecticut*,	Classical Oration
John Bayard McPherson, *Pennsylvania*,	Philosophical Oration
William F. C Morsell, *Delaware*,	Philosophical Oration
Robert C Dalzell, *West Virginia*,	Physical Oration
Roger W. Butterfield, *New Jersey*,	Physical Oration

JUNIOR ORATORS
Cliosophic Society

William Frame,	*New Jersey*
William Rossman Henderson,	*Indiana*
James Gibson Lowrie,	*Indiana*
Charles Benjamin Ogilvie,	*Iowa*

---

[1] Medals were first awarded at this contest (1865)

[2] The minutes of the Faculty divide the honors into two classes, the first and highest comprise the special Honorary Orations, the second, the Honorary Speeches   Hereafter only the former, which are distinctively the high honors, and others, if of equal standing, will be included in this list

[3] Bergner and Sherrill equal in scholarship, average 98.9   *Minutes of the Faculty*, May 18, 1866

American Whig Society

Robert Forsyth Little,	*New York*
Samuel Moody Murphey,	*Delaware*
James Boyd Nixon,	*New Jersey*
William Henry Thompson,	*Pennsylvania*

Junior Orator Medalists

William Frame,	First Medal
James Gibson Lowrie,	Second Medal
Samuel Moody Murphey,	Third Medal
Charles Benjamin Ogilvie,	Fourth Medal

1867

Richard Wayne Parker,[1] *New Jersey*,	Valedictory Oration
Lewis French Stearns, *New Jersey*,	Latin Salutatory
Oliver Maclean Green,[2] *Pennsylvania*,	English Salutatory
Francis Elston Marsh, *New Jersey*,	Physical Oration
George Rigg, *New Jersey*,	Mathematical Oration
Arthur Rutherford Morris, *New York*,	Philosophical Oration
William Mindred Johnson,[3] *New Jersey*,	Classical Oration
Richard Garrison Stretch, *New Jersey*,	Philosophical Oration
John Watkins Swarts, *New Jersey*,	Metaphysical Oration
Joseph Lewis Potter, *Indiana*,	Physical Oration
James Gibson Lowrie,[4] *Indiana*,	Belles Lettres Oration

Caleb Hunn Rodney,	*Delaware*

JUNIOR ORATORS

Cliosophic Society

Alfred Hamilton Fahnestock,	*Illinois*
Samuel Miller Hageman,	*New Jersey*
Huston Humphreys,	*Maryland*
Archibald McCullagh,	*New Jersey*

[1] Parker and Stearns equal in scholarship, average 99 1   *Minutes of the Faculty*, May 17, 1867

[2] Green and Marsh equal, average 98 4   *Ibid*

[3] Johnson and Stretch equal, average 97 5   *Ibid*

[4] Lowrie and Rodney equal, average 96 6.   *Ibid.*

American Whig Society

Edward Cleves Hood,	*New Jersey*
Dallas Valentine Mays,	*Pennsylvania*
Alexander Robinson Pendleton,	*Virginia*
Eli Marsh Turner,	*Virginia*

Junior Orator Medalists

Alfred Hamilton Fahnestock, } *Equal,*   First Medal
Edward Cleves Hood,

Samuel Miller Hageman, } *Equal,*   Second Medal
Alexander Robinson Pendleton,

1868

Edward Hyde Robbins, *Maryland,*	Latin Salutatory
Alfred Hamilton Fahnestock, *Illinois,*	English Salutatory
Eli Marsh Turner, *Virginia,*	Valedictory Oration
Charles Sidney Converse,[1] *Virginia,*	Classical (Latin) Oration
William Cooper Rommel, *New Jersey,*	Classical (Greek) Oration
James Madison Poulson,[2] *Ohio,*	Philosophical Oration
Alexander Robinson Pendleton, *Virginia,*	Belles Lettres Oration
William Scott, *Pennsylvania,*	Philosophical Oration
Charles Edward Pierson, *New Jersey,*	Physical Oration
Elwood Cummins Harris,[3] *New Jersey,*	Mathematical Oration
Henry Pleasant Fowlkes, *Tennessee,*	Philosophical Oration

JUNIOR ORATORS

Cliosophic Society

John William Aitkin,	*New York*
John Frelinghuysen Hageman, Jr.,	*New Jersey*
James McLeod,	*Ireland*
Eugene Franklin Wells,	*New York*

---

[1] Converse and Rommel equal in scholarship, average 97 8   *Minutes of the Faculty,* April 30, 1868

[2] Poulson and Pendleton equal, average 97 3   *Ibid*

[3] Harris and Fowlkes equal, average 96 6   *Ibid*

American Whig Society

James Thomas Finley,	*Alabama*
John Patton Irvin,	*Pennsylvania*
William Henry Park	*Ohio*
Winfield Scott Stites,	*New Jersey*

Junior Orator Medalists

James McLeod,	First Medal
James Thomas Finley,	Second Medal
Winfield Scott Stites,	Third Medal
William Henry Park,	Fourth Medal

1869

Senior Honors

Archibald Alexander Schenck, *Pennsylvania*,	Latin Salutatory
Edward Quinton Keasbey, *New Jersey*,	English Salutatory
Richard Boyd Webster, *Pennsylvania*,	Metaphysical Oration
Alexander Speer, *District of Columbia*,	Belles Lettres Oration
Thomas Allen Jobs,[1] *New Jersey*,	Classical Oration
John William Rosebro, *North Carolina*,	Valedictory Oration
Nathaniel Ewing, Jr., *Pennsylvania*,	Philosophical Oration
William Henry Park,[2] *Ohio*,	Philosophical Oration
Henry Clay Talmage, *New York*,	Philosophical Oration
Jonas Turner Brakeley, *New Jersey*,	Physical Oration

PRIZEMEN

George Potts Bible Prizes

Edward Quinton Keasbey,	*New Jersey*
Richard Boyd Webster,	*Pennsylvania*

Junior Honors

Theodoric Bland Pryor, *New York*,	First Honor

---

[1] Jobs and Rosebro equal, average 96 8   *Minutes of the Faculty*, May 17, 1869

[2] Park and Talmage equal, average 96 5   *Ibid*

Junior Orators

Cliosophic Society

William M Bartholomew,	*Indiana*
Adrian Hoffman Joline,	*New York*
Asher Brown Temple,	*New Jersey*
George Conrad Yeisley,	*Maryland*

American Whig Society

John Crawford,	*Delaware*
Hugh Graham Kyle,	*Tennessee*
William Pitt Schell, Jr ,	*Pennsylvania*
Emelius W. Smith,	*Pennsylvania*

Junior Orator Medalists

Asher Brown Temple,	First Medal
George Conrad Yeisley,	Second Medal
John Crawford,	Third Medal
Emelius W Smith,	Fourth Medal

Fellows

Boudinot Fellow in Belles Lettres and Philosophy

Theodore Whitefield Hunt, '65.	*New Jersey*

Boudinot Fellow in Latin

John Howard O'Brien, '64,	*Nova Scotia*

Boudinot Fellow in Mathematics

Fuller Porter Dalrymple, '67,	*New Jersey*

1870

Senior Honors

Theodoric Bland Pryor, *New York*,	Latin Salutatory
William Hamilton Miller, *Pennsylvania*,	Greek Salutatory
Elmer Ewing Green, *New Jersey*,	English Salutatory
Stevenson Archer Williams, *Maryland*,	Metaphysical Oration
Hugh Graham Kyle, *Tennessee*,	Valedictory Oration
George Heberton Hooper, *New Jersey*,	Classical Oration

John Ellsworth Peters,[1] *New Jersey,*		Physical Oration
John Todd Shelby, *Kentucky,*		Historical Oration
Abner Bailey Kelly, *District of Columbia,*		Classical Oration
George Conrad Yeisley, *Maryland,*		Belles Lettres Oration
Adrian Hoffman Joline, *New York,*		Literary Oration
Emelius W. Smith, *Pennsylvania,*		Philosophical Oration
Joseph Thomas Kelly, *District of Columbia,* Philosophical Oration
Gardner Clinton Deaver,[2] *Pennsylvania,*	Mathematical Oration
James William McIlvaine, *Maryland,*		Classical Oration
Charles Albert Reynolds,			*North Carolina*
Alexander Henry, Jr , *Pennsylvania,*		Ethical Oration
Charles James Roe,[3]			*New Jersey*
David Robert Sessions, *South Carolina,*

					Modern Language Oration
Mark Reeves Sooy,				*New Jersey*
Elias M Pennington,				*New Jersey*
John Van Vorst, Jr.,				*New Jersey*
Charles Hampton Moore,[4]			*Pennsylvania*
David Junkin Satterfield,			*Pennsylvania*
Charles Frederick Imbrie,[5] *New Jersey,*		Literary Oration
Frank Addison Ward,				*New York*

FELLOWS

Jay Cooke Fellow in Mathematics
Theodoric Bland Pryor,				*New York*

Field Fellow in Classical Literature
George Heberton Hooper,				*New Jersey*

Fellow in Mental Science
William Davy Thomas,				*Wales*

[1] Peters and Shelby equal in scholarship, average 98 1   *Minutes of the Faculty,* June 16, 1870

[2] Deaver and McIlvaine equal, average 97   *Ibid*

[3] Roe and Sessions equal, average 96 4   *Ibid*

[4] Moore and Satterfield equal, average 95 3   *Ibid*

[5] Imbrie and Ward equal, average 94 8.   *Ibid*

PRIZEMEN

Experimental Science Prize

William Hamilton Miller,   *Pennsylvania*

Class of 1859 Prize in English Literature

Charles Frederick Imbrie,[1]   *New Jersey*
David Robert Sessions,   *South Carolina*
George Conrad Yeisley,   *Maryland*

George Potts Bible Prizes

John Ellsworth Peters,   *New Jersey*
Emelius W Smith,   *Pennsylvania*

Junior Honors

Benjamin Breckinridge Warfield, *Kentucky*,   First Honor

JUNIOR ORATORS

Cliosophic Society

Frederick K. Castner,   *New York*
Oliver Alexander Kerr,   *Pennsylvania*
Joseph Angelo Owen,   *New Jersey*
Josephus Leander Sooy,   *New Jersey*

American Whig Society

Hugh Henderson Hamill,   *New Jersey*
Louis Henry Mayers,   *Ohio*
Edward I Todd,   *Pennsylvania*
John G. Weir,   *Kentucky*

Junior Orator Medalists

Hugh Henderson Hamill, ⎱ *Equal,*
Frederick K. Castner,   ⎰   First Medal
Oliver Alexander Kerr,   Third Medal
Louis Henry Mayers,   Fourth Medal

---

[1] Imbrie, Sessions, and Yeisley equal. *Honor List, 1870*

1871

Senior Honors

Benjamin Breckinridge Warfield, *Kentucky*,	Latin Salutatory
Alexander Green Van Cleve, *New Jersey*,	English Salutatory
Charles Scudder Barrett,[1] *New Jersey*,	Metaphysical Oration
William McDowell Halsey, *New York*,	Mathematical Oration
John Laird, *Pennsylvania*,	Valedictory Oration
Josephus Leander Sooy, *New Jersey*,	Rhetorical Oration
Oliver Alexander Kerr, *Pennsylvania*,	Philosophical Oration
Henry Wyre Scudder, *Georgia*,	Philosophical Oration
Benjamin Skinner Lassiter,[2] *North Carolina*,	Classical Oration
Samuel Mustard Perry, *Delaware*,	Philosophical Oration
Charles Kisselman Imbrie Miller,	*Pennsylvania*
Homer Davenport Boughner,[3]	*West Virginia*
William Butler Hornblower, *New Jersey*,	Literary Oration
William Tuttle Carter,	*New Jersey*
Roswell Randall Hoes,[4]	*New York*
Frederick Aycrigg Pell, *New Jersey*,	Modern Language Oration
Charles Kingsbury Westbrook, *Pennsylvania*,	
	Classical (Greek) Oration
Charles Winters Darst,[5]	*Ohio*
Andrew Patton Happer, Jr.,	*China*
Albert Brainerd Marshall,	*Pennsylvania*
Joseph Angelo Owen, *New Jersey*,	Historical Oration

Fellows

Jay Cooke Fellow in Mathematics

Alexander Green Van Cleve,	*New Jersey*

---

[1] Barrett and Halsey equal, average 98 *Minutes of the Faculty*, June 17, 1871

[2] Lassiter and Perry equal, average 95 6 *Ibid*

[3] Boughner and Hornblower equal, average 94.2. *Ibid.*

[4] Hoes, Pell, and Westbrook equal, average 93 5 *Ibid*

[5] Darst and Happer equal, average 93 2 *Ibid*

Marquand Fellow in Classical Literature

Benjamin Skinner Lassiter,   *North Carolina*

Chancellor Green Fellow in Mental Science

Charles Scudder Barrett,   *New Jersey*

Class of 1860 Fellow in Experimental Science

John Condit Pennington,   *New Jersey*

Prizemen

Class of 1859 Prize in English Literature

William Butler Hornblower,   *New Jersey*

George Potts Bible Prizes

Chauncey Mitchell Field,   *New Jersey*
Albert Brainerd Marshall,   *Pennsylvania*

Junior Honors

Leigh Richmond Smith, *Alabama*,   First Honor

Junior Orators

Cliosophic Society

Franklin Pease Berry,   *New Jersey*
Addison Lowell Daniels,   *Iowa*
Frederick Beal Du Val,   *Maryland*
Chester Paul Murray,   *Ohio*

American Whig Society

Addison Atwater,   *New Jersey*
John Clarence Lane,   *Maryland*
Winfied Robert Martin,   *China*
George Wilson,   *Pennsylvania*

Junior Orator Medalists

Addison Lowell Daniels, ⎫
                                  ⎬ *Equal,*   First Medal
John Clarence Lane,   ⎭

Franklin Pease Berry,   } *Equal,*   Second Medal
Winfred Robert Martin,   }

1872

Leigh Richmond Smith, *Alabama,*	Latin Salutatory
James Adair Lyon, Jr.,[1] *Mississippi,*	English Salutatory
Richmond Pearson, *North Carolina,*	Valedictory Oration
John Crawford, *Delaware,*	Philosophical Oration
Henry Nevius Van Dyke, *New Jersey,*	Classical (Greek) Oration
Cornelius Suydam Scott, *Kentucky,*	Metaphysical Oration
Melbert Brinkerhoff Cary, *Wisconsin,*	Physical Oration
John Clarence Lane, *Maryland,*	Rhetorical Oration
Walter Reuben Frame, *Illinois,*	Mathematical Oration
George Augustus Blake, *New Jersey,*	Political Science Oration
Samuel Evans Ewing, *Pennsylvania,*	Classical Oration

FELLOWS

Jay Cooke Fellow in Mathematics

James Adair Lyon, Jr.,   *Mississippi*

Marquand Fellow in Classical Literature

Winfred Robert Martin,   *China*

Chancellor Green Fellow in Mental Science

Leigh Richmond Smith,   *Alabama*

Class of 1860 Fellow in Experimental Science

Albert Williams, Jr ,   *New Jersey*

Boudinot Fellow in Modern Languages

John Hitchcock Scribner,   *New Jersey*

Boudinot Fellow in History

James Forsyth Riggs,   *Turkey*

---

[1] Lyon and Pearson equal in scholarship, average 98 4   *Minutes of the Faculty,* June 14, 1872

PRIZEMEN

Class of 1859 Prize in English Literature

Isaac Davison Decker,   *New Jersey*

George Potts Bible Prizes

Arthur Nuel Bruen,   *New Jersey*
Frederick Beal Du Val,   *Maryland*

Junior Honors

John P. Kennedy Bryan, *South Carolina*,   First Honor

JUNIOR ORATORS

Cliosophic Society

John P. Kennedy Bryan,   *South Carolina*
George Howard Duffield,   *New Jersey*
Simon John McPherson,   *New York*
Henry Jackson Van Dyke, Jr ,   *Tennessee*

American Whig Society

Josiah Robert Adams,   *New Jersey*
Artemas Bissell,   *New York*
James Hoagland Cowen,   *Ohio*
Herman Haupt North,   *Pennsylvania*

Junior Orator Medalists

Josiah Robert Adams,   First Medal
George Howard Duffield,   Second Medal
Henry Jackson Van Dyke, Jr.,   Third Medal
John P. Kennedy Bryan,   Fourth Medal

PRIZEMEN

Maclean Prize

Simon John McPherson,   *New York*

Dickinson Prize

George Stockton Burroughs,   *Pennsylvania*

Sophomore Honors
Class of 1861 Prize

George Henry Ferris, *Michigan*

1873
Senior Honors

John P Kennedy Bryan, *South Carolina*,   Valedictory Oration
George Stockton Burroughs, *Pennsylvania*,   Latin Salutatory
Henry Jackson Van Dyke, Jr., *Tennessee*,   English Salutatory
and the Belles Lettres Oration
Isaac Hiram Condit,[1] *New Jersey*,   Mathematical Oration
David Scott, Jr , *New York*,   Classical Oration
Samuel McLanahan, *Pennsylvania*,   Metaphysical Oration
Joseph Heatly Dulles, Jr , *Pennsylvania*,
Modern Language Oration
George Howard Duffield, *New Jersey*,   Philosophical Oration
Thomas Hoff Rittenhouse,[2] *New Jersey*,
Political Science Oration
William Ward Van Valzah, *Pennsylvania*,
Second Classical Oration
John Ewing Speer,   *Pennsylvania*
John Crocker Fisher, *New York*,   Physical Oration

FELLOWS

Marquand Fellow in Classical Literature

David Scott, Jr.,   *New York*

Chancellor Green Fellow in Mental Science

John P. Kennedy Bryan,   *South Carolina*

Class of 1860 Fellow in Experimental Science

Walter Bourchier Devereux,   *New York*

---

[1] Condit and Scott of equal scholarship, average 97 5   *Minutes of the Faculty*, June 19, 1873

[2] Rittenhouse and Van Valzah equal, average 95.3. *Ibid*

Boudinot Fellow in Modern Languages

John Jackson Hubbell,   *New Jersey*

Boudinot Fellow in History

Clifton Ferguson Cair,   *Kentucky*

Prizemen

Class of 1859 Prize in English Literature

Henry Jackson Van Dyke, Jr.,   *Tennessee*

George Potts Bible Prizes

George Howard Duffield,   *New Jersey*
George Stockton Burroughs,   *Pennsylvania*

Science and Religion Prize

Josiah Robert Adams,   *New Jersey*

Political Science Prize

George Opdyke Vanderbilt,   *New Jersey*

Junior Honors

Samuel Ross Winans, Jr., *New Jersey*,   First Honor

Junior Orators
Cliosophic Society

Richard Edgar Field,   *New Jersey*
Harry Murray Hinckley,   *Pennsylvania*
Walter Douglass Nicholas,   *New Jersey*
Willis Hulette Wiggins,   *New York*

American Whig Society

James Stevenson Riggs,   *New York*
James Henry Ross,   *New York*
Nathaniel Irwin Rubinkam, Jr ,   *Pennsylvania*
William Henry Sponsler,   *Pennsylvania*

Junior Orator Medalists

James Henry Ross,	First Medal
William Henry Sponsler,	Second Medal
Walter Douglass Nicholas,	Third Medal
Willis Hulette Wiggins,	Fourth Medal

PRIZEMEN

Maclean Prize

James Henry Ross,	*New York*

Dickinson Prize

Andrew Fleming West,	*Kentucky*

In English Literature

Charles Fauntleroy Whittlesey,	*Virginia*

In French Literature

Allan Marquand,	*New York*

Sophomore Honors

Biennial Prizeman

John P. Campbell,	*New York*

Stinnecke Scholar

Ellsworth Eliot Hunt,	*New Jersey*

Class of 1861 Prize

Frederick Boyd Van Vorst,	*New York*

Freshman Honors

Albert Van Deusen, *New York*,	First Honor

1874

Senior Honors

Simon John McPherson, *New York*,	English Salutatory
Allan Marquand,[1] *New York*,	Latin Salutatory
Samuel Ross Winans, Jr , *New Jersey*,	Greek Salutatory
Charles Fauntleroy Whittlesey, *Virginia*,	Valedictory Oration
William Thomas Wilson, *Indiana*,	Modern Language Oration
George Henry Ferris,[2] *Michigan*,	Mathematical and Physical Oration
James Stevenson Riggs, *New York*,	Classical (Greek) Oration
James Julius Chisholm, *South Carolina*,	Philosophical Oration
Alexander Reid Whitehill, *Pennsylvania*,	Geological Oration
Andrew Fleming West, *Kentucky*,	Classical Oration
Henry Elliott Mott,[3] *Michigan*,	Belles Lettres Oration
De Lancey Nicoll, *New York*,	Belles Lettres Oration

Fellows

Marquand Fellow in Classical Literature

Andrew Fleming West,   *Kentucky*

J S K Fellow in Mathematics

George Henry Ferris,   *Michigan*

Chancellor Green Fellow in Mental Science

Samuel Ross Winans, Jr ,   *New Jersey*

Class of 1860 Fellow in Experimental Science

Alexander Reid Whitehill,   *Pennsylvania*

Boudinot Fellow in Modern Languages

David Compton,   *New Jersey*

---

[1] Marquand and Winans equal in scholarship, average 98 8 *Minutes of the Faculty*, June 12, 1874

[2] Ferris and Riggs equal, average 97 4   *Ibid*

[3] Mott and Nicoll equal, average 96. *Ibid.*

Boudinot Fellow in History

John Wesley Gephart,   *Pennsylvania*

PRIZEMEN

Class of 1859 Prize in English Literature

De Lancey Nicoll,   *New York*

George Potts Bible Prizes

James Julius Chisholm,   *South Carolina*
John Graham Reid,   *New York*

Science and Religion Prize

Allan Marquand,   *New York*

Political Science

Thomas Henry Atherton,   *Pennsylvania*

Junior Honors

Gustav Adolf Endlich, *Pennsylvania*,   First Honor

JUNIOR ORATORS

Cliosophic Society

John P Campbell,   *New York*
John Patterson Coyle,   *Pennsylvania*
George Bruce Halsted,   *New Jersey*
James Pennewill,   *Delaware*

American Whig Society

Charles Claflin Allen,   *Missouri*
Samuel Millington Miller,   *Pennsylvania*
Arthur Newman,   *New York*
Dudley Goodall Wooten,   *Texas*

Junior Orator Medalists

Arthur Newman,   First Medal
Dudley Goodall Wooten,   Second Medal

John P Campbell,   Third Medal
James Pennewill,   Fourth Medal

PRIZEMEN
Maclean Prize
James Pennewill,   *Delaware*

Dickinson Prize
Arthur Newman,   *New York*

In English Literature
Archibald Alexander,   *New York*

In French Literature
Gustav Adolf Endlich,   *Pennsylvania*

In Mental Science
Archibald Alexander,   *New York*

Stinnecke Scholar
Ellsworth Eliot Hunt,   *New Jersey*

Sophomore Honors
Biennial Prizeman
William Brenton Greene, Jr ,   *Rhode Island*

Class of 1861 Prize
Chandler White Riker,   *New Jersey*

Classical Prizeman
William Edgar Plumley,   *New York*

SCHOOL OF SCIENCE
Prize in Chemistry
Howard Russell Butler,   *New York*

Freshman Honors
Adrian Riker, *New Jersey*,   First Honor

Freshman Entrance Prize

William Berryman Scott,   *New Jersey*

1875

Senior Honors

Charles Richard Williams, *New York*,	Latin Salutatory
Ellsworth Eliot **Hunt**, *New Jersey*,	English Salutatory
John P Campbell, *New York*,	Valedictory Oration
Arthur Newman, *New York*,	Greek Salutatory
Gustav Adolph Endlich, *Pennsylvania*,	German Salutatory

William Vanzandt Louderbough, *Delaware*,

Philosophical Oration

Walter Hunnewell Underwood, *New York*,

Modern Language Oration

John Patterson Coyle,[1] *Pennsylvania*,	Physical Oration
John Smith Plumer, *Pennsylvania*,	Honorary Oration
Charles Scribner, *New York*,	Metaphysical Oration
Charles Mowry Fleming, *Pennsylvania*,	Honorary Oration
William Sanderson Cheesman, Jr., *New York*,	Honorary Oration
Allen Macy Dulles, *Pennsylvania*,	Honorary Oration
John McElmoyle, *Maryland*,	Belles Lettres Oration
George Bruce Halsted, *New Jersey*,	Mathematical Oration

Fellows

Marquand Fellow in Classical Literature

Charles Richard Williams,   *New York*

J S K Fellow in Mathematics

George Bruce Halsted,   *New Jersey*

Chancellor Green Fellows in Mental Science

Frederick Boyd Van Vorst,	*New York*
Archibald Alexander,	*New York*

[1] Coyle, Plumer, and Scribner of equal scholarship, average 95 7   *Minutes of the Faculty,* June 17, 1875

Class of 1860 Fellow in Experimental Science

Ellsworth Eliot Hunt,   *New Jersey*

Boudinot Fellow in Modern Languages

John McElmoyle,   *Maryland*

Boudinot Fellow in History

Dudley Goodall Wooten,   *Texas*

Prizemen

Class of 1859 Prize in English Literature

John McElmoyle,   *Maryland*

Science and Religion Prize

Allen Macy Dulles,   *Pennsylvania*

Political Science Prize

Patterson Andrews Reece,   *Ohio*

Junior Honors

David Benton Jones,[1] *Wisconsin,*
Thomas Davies Jones, *Wisconsin,*   First Honor

Junior Orators
Clıosophıc Socıety

John Fletcher Duffield,   *New Jersey*
William James Henderson,   *New Jersey*
David Benton Jones,   *Wisconsin*
Albert Van Deusen,   *New York*

American Whig Society

Henry Edgar Davis,   *District of Columbia*
William Brenton Greene, Jr ,   *Rhode Island*

---

[1] D B Jones and T B Jones equal in scholarship, average 99 7 *Minutes of the Faculty*, June 18, 1875

James Walter Lowrie,   *New York*
Leonard Walter Lott,   *New York*

Junior Orator Medalists

James Walter Lowrie,   First Medal
Henry Edgar Davis,   Second Medal
John Fletcher Duffield,   Third Medal
Albert Van Deusen,   Fourth Medal

PRIZEMEN

Maclean Prize

Henry Edgar Davis,   *District of Columbia*

Dickinson Prize

George Black Stewart,   *Ohio*

In English Literature

Thomas Davies Jones,   *Wisconsin*

In French Literature

Moses Allen Starr,   *New Jersey*

In Mental Science

Thomas Davies Jones,   *Wisconsin*

Sophomore Honors

Biennial Prizeman

Adrian Riker,   *New Jersey*

Class of 1861 Prize

Malcolm McNeill,   *Illinois*

Classical Prizeman

Hugh Silas Stuart,   *Pennsylvania*

Freshman Honors

Herbert Stearns Squier Smith, *New Jersey*,   First Honor

Freshman Entrance Prizeman
Robert Atkinson Mayo,   *New York*

1876

Senior Honors

David Benton Jones,[1] *Wisconsin*,   Latin Salutatory
Thomas Davies Jones, *Wisconsin*,   English Salutatory
Moses Allen Starr, *New Jersey*,   Philosophical Oration
William Brenton Greene, Jr , *Rhode Island*, Valedictory Oration
Alexander Russell Stevenson, *Pennsylvania*,

                                            Philosophical Oration
Albert Van Deusen, *New York*,   Modern Language Oration
Henry Alfred Todd, *Illinois*,   Belles Lettres Oration
Frederick Alexander Marquand, *New York*,

                                             Belles Lettres Oration
Chandler White Riker, *New Jersey*,   Mathematical Oration
Charles Brookes Chapin,[2] *New York*,   Classical Oration
Edward Charles Evans, *Pennsylvania*,   Mental Science Oration

SCHOOL OF SCIENCE

Howard Russell Butler, *New York*,   First Honor

FELLOWS

Marquand Fellow in Classical Literature
Edward Charles Evans,   *Pennsylvania*

J S K Fellow in Mathematics
Chandler White Riker,   *New Jersey*

Chancellor Green Fellow in Mental Science
Thomas Davies Jones,   *Wisconsin*

[1] D B Jones and T D Jones of equal scholarship, average 99 2.   *Minutes of the Faculty*, June 15, 1876.

[2] Chapin and Evans equal, average 96 5   *Ibid*

Class of 1860 Fellow in Experimental Science

David Benton Jones, *Wisconsin*

Boudinot Fellow in Modern Languages

Henry Alfred Todd, *Illinois*

Boudinot Fellows in History

William Allen Butler, *New York*
Clarence Cunningham, *South Carolina*

Prizemen

Class of 1859 Prize in English Literature

Moses Allen Starr, *New Jersey*

George Potts Bible Prizes

Sylvester Woodbridge Beach, *Maryland*
John Pollock Brown, *New York*

Science and Religion Prize

George Black Stewart, *Ohio*

Lynde Prize Debate

Cliosophic Society

James Morrison Barkley, *North Carolina*
David Benton Jones, *Wisconsin*
Thomas Davies Jones, *Wisconsin*

American Whig Society

Henry Edgar Davis, *District of Columbia*
Collins Denny, *Virginia*
William Brenton Greene, Jr., *Rhode Island*

Lynde Debate Prizemen

David Benton Jones, First Prize
William Brenton Greene, Jr , Second Prize
James Morrison Barkley, Third Prize

Junior Honors

William Berryman Scott, *New Jersey*,   First Honor

Junior Orators
Cliosophic Society

Robert McCheyne Mateer,   *Pennsylvania*
Samuel James Rowland,   *New York*
Wilton Merle Smith,   *New York*
Luther Deloraine Wishard,   *Indiana*

American Whig Society

Wilhelmus Bogart Bryan,   *Pennsylvania*
William Fullerton Dunning,   *New York*
Alexander Thomas Ormond,   *Pennsylvania*
William Emmett Slemmons,   *Ohio*

Junior Orator Medalists

Wilton Merle Smith,   First Medal
William Emmett Slemmons,   Second Medal
Samuel James Rowland,   Third Medal
William Fullerton Dunning,   Fourth Medal

Prizemen
Maclean Prize

William Emmett Slemmons,   *Ohio*

Dickinson Prize

Jotham Potter,   *Ohio*

Sophomore Honors
Stinnecke Scholar

David Stewart,   *Maryland*

Class of 1861 Prize

John Richard Van Benschoten,   *Connecticut*

Classical Prize

Francis Stoddard Haines,   *New Jersey*

Freshman Honors

John D Davis, *Pennsylvania,*   }
William Francis Magie, *New Jersey,* } *Equal,*   First Honor

Freshman Entrance Prize

William Francis Magie,   *New Jersey*

1877

Senior Honors

Malcolm McNeill,[1] *Illinois,*   Latin Salutatory
William Berryman Scott, *New Jersey,*   English Salutatory
John Howell Westcott, *Pennsylvania,*   Classical Oration
William Emmett Slemmons, *Ohio,*   Valedictory Oration
Samuel Bratton, *Maryland,*   Physical Oration
Ira Wells Wood, *New Jersey,*   Philosophical Oration
Frederick Campbell, *New York,*   Ethical Oration
Walter Hazard, *South Carolina,*   English Literature Oration
Hugh Silas Stuart, *Pennsylvania,*   Philosophical Oration
Daniel Bratton, Jr , *Maryland,*   Philosophical Oration
James Franklin Williamson, *Ohio,*   Geological Oration
Melancthon Williams Jacobus, Jr ,[2] *Pennsylvania,*

                                                     Honorary Oration
Alexander Thomas Ormond, *Pennsylvania,*

                                                Mental Science Oration
John Moore, *New Jersey,*   Honorary Oration
Henry Cooper Pitney, *New Jersey,*   Modern Language Oration
Walter Lloyd Smith, *New York,*   Honorary Oration
Andrew James McCosh, *New Jersey,*   Modern Language Oration
Richard Wilde Walker, Jr , *Alabama,*   Honorary Oration
John Hood Laughlin, *Pennsylvania,*   Honorary Oration

----

[1] McNeill and Scott equal in scholarship, average 97 7 *Minutes of the Faculty,* June 5, 1877

[2] Jacobus and Ormond equal, average 93 7   *Ibid*

Jerome Thompson Ailman,[1] *Pennsylvania*,   Honorary Oration
Carl Leopold Spethman, *Germany*,   Honorary Oration
William Clinton Armstrong, *New Jersey*,   Honorary Oration
John Alexander Campbell, *District of Columbia*,
                                               Honorary Oration
George Henry Gowdy, *Kentucky*,   Mathematical Oration

School of Science Honormen

Donald Fraser McPherson, *New York*,   First Honor
Henry Burling Thompson, *Pennsylvania*,   Second Honor
Henry Dwight Chapin, *New York*,   Third Honor

Fellows

Marquand Fellow in Classical Literature
John Howell Westcott,   *Pennsylvania*

J. S. K. Fellow in Mathematics[2]
George Henry Gowdy,   *Kentucky*

Chancellor Green Fellow in Mental Science
Alexander Thomas Ormond,   *Pennsylvania*

Class of 1860 Fellow in Experimental Science
William Berryman Scott,   *New Jersey*

Boudinot Fellow in Modern Languages
Henry Cooper Pitney,   *New Jersey*

Boudinot Fellow in History
Richard Wilde Walker, Jr.,   *Alabama*

S. L. Fellows in Mental and Social Science
James Franklin Williamson,   *Ohio*
John B. Wardlaw,   *Georgia*

---

[1] Ailman and Spethman equal, average 92.1   *Minutes of the Faculty*, June 5, 1877

[2] With honorable mention of Malcolm McNeill of Illinois

Prizemen

Class of 1859 Prize in English Literature

John B Wardlaw,   *Georgia*

George Potts Bible Prizes

James Creighton Hume,   *Maryland*
John Hood Laughlin,   *Pennsylvania*

Science and Religion Prize

Frederick Campbell,   *New York*

Lynde Prize Debate

Cliosophic Society

Samuel James Rowland,   *New York*
Walter Lloyd Smith,   *New York*
James Franklin Williamson,   *Ohio*

American Whig Society

William Emmett Slemmons,   *Ohio*
Hugh Silas Stuart,   *Pennsylvania*
John B. Wardlaw,   *Georgia*

Lynde Debate Prizemen

Samuel James Rowland,   First Prize
Hugh Silas Stuart,   Second Prize
John B. Wardlaw,   Third Prize

Junior Honors

Albert Duy Anderson, *New Jersey*,   First Honor

Junior Orators

Cliosophic Society

William W. McDonald,   *New York*
William Duncan Van Dyke,   *Wisconsin*

Charles Luther Williams,   *New Jersey*
Abram Heebner Wintersteen,   *Pennsylvania*

American Whig Society

Albert Webster Dickens,   *New York*
William Dulles, Jr ,   *Pennsylvania*
Robert Atkinson Mayo,   *New York*
David Stewart,   *Maryland*

Junior Orator Medalists

Charles Luther Williams,   First Medal
Albert Webster Dickens,   Second Medal
William W. McDonald,   Third Medal
William Duncan Van Dyke,   Fourth Medal

Prizemen
Maclean Prize

William Dulles, Jr ,   *Pennsylvania*

Dickinson Prize

Henry Marquand,   *New York*

Stinnecke Scholar

David Stewart,   *Maryland*

Sophomore Honors

John D Davis, *Pennsylvania*,   First Honor

Stinnecke Prizemen

John D. Davis,   *Pennsylvania*
William Francis Magie,   *New Jersey*
Donald Campbell McLaren,   *New Jersey*

Class of 1861 Prize

Fletcher Durell,   *New Jersey*

Freshman Honors

Henry Burchard Fine, *Minnesota,*   First Honor

L. of C.

1878

Senior Honors

Albert Duy Anderson, *New Jersey*,	Latin Salutatory
David Stewart, *Maryland*,	Valedictory Oration
George William Kretsinger, *California*,	English Salutatory
George Riggs Gaithei, Jr , *Maryland*,	Philosophical Oration
Robert Atkinson Mayo, *New York*,	Philological Oration
Thomas Cumming Beattie, *New Jersey*,	Classical Oration
David Mitchell Leib, *Pennsylvania*,	Physical Oration
Richard Lenox Halsey,[1] *New York*,	Classical Oration
Isaac Hiester Hess, *Maryland*,	Mathematical Oration
Abram Heebner Wintersteen, *Pennsylvania*,	
	English Literature Oration
Henry Marquand, *New York*,	Philosophical Oration
William Dulles, Jr., *Pennsylvania*,	Ethical Oration

Leroy Wiley McCay, *Maryland*,　　Modern Language Oration

School of Science Honormen

Herbert Stearns Squier Smith, *New Jersey*,	First Honor
Elisha Kent Kane, *Pennsylvania*,	Second Honor
Charles Day Bennett, *New Jersey*,	Third Honor

Fellows

Marquand Fellow in Classical Literature

Robert Atkinson Mayo,　　　　　　　　　　*New York*

J S. K Fellow in Mathematics

Isaac Hiester Hess,　　　　　　　　　　　*Maryland*

Chancellor Green Fellow in Mental Science

David Stewart,　　　　　　　　　　　　　*Maryland*

---

[1] Halsey and Hess equal in scholarship, average 94.2　*Minutes of the Faculty*, June 1, 1878

Class of 1860 Fellow in Experimental Science

Albert Duy Anderson,   *New Jersey*

Boudinot Fellow in Modern Languages

William Terrell Dawson,   *Maryland*

S L Fellows in Mental and Social Science

George William Kretsinger,   *California*
Alexander Thomas Ormond, '77,   *Pennsylvania*
James Franklin Williamson, '77,   *Ohio*

E M Fellow in Physical Science

Malcolm McNeill, '77,   *Illinois*

In Geological Science

William Berryman Scott, '77,   *New Jersey*

Prizemen

Class of 1859 Prize in English Literature[1]

Abram Heebner Wintersteen,   *Pennsylvania*

George Potts Bible Prize

William Tenton Kruse,   *Pennsylvania*
George Stephen Munson,   *Pennsylvania*

Science and Religion Prize

Francis Stoddard Haines,   *New Jersey*

Lynde Prize Debate

Cliosophic Society

Thomas Cumming Beattie,   *New Jersey*
Willard Scoullar McEachron,   *New York*
Abram Heebner Wintersteen,   *Pennsylvania*

---

[1] With honorable mention of Richard Arnold Greene of Rhode Island

American Whig Society

Preston Barr,	*Pennsylvania*
William Dulles, Jr ,	*Pennsylvania*
George William Kretsinger,	*California*

Lynde Debate Prizemen

Willard Scoullar McEachron,	First Prize
Preston Barr,	Second Prize
William Dulles, Jr ,	Third Prize

Junior Honors

John D. Davis, *Pennsylvania*,	First Honor

JUNIOR ORATORS

Cliosophic Society

Andrew Allen Chambers,	*New Jersey*
Harold Godwin,	*New York*
Abram Woodruff Halsey,	*New Jersey*
Chalmers Martin,	*New Jersey*

American Whig Society

John D. Davis,	*Pennsylvania*
William Thaddeus Elsing,	*Illinois*
Samuel Allen Harlow,	*New York*
Robert Harris McCarter,	*New Jersey*

Junior Orator Medalists

William Thaddeus Elsing,	First Medal
Chalmers Martin,	Second Medal
Andrew Allen Chambers,	Third Medal
Samuel Allen Harlow,	Fourth Medal

PRIZEMEN

Maclean Prize

William Thaddeus Elsing,	*Illinois*

Dickinson Prize

William Francis Magie,   *New Jersey*

Sophomore Honors

Henry Burchard Fine, *Minnesota*,   First Honor

Stinnecke Prizemen

Henry Burchard Fine,   *Minnesota*
Cæsar Augustus Rodney Janvier,   *India*
James Dunlop Paxton,   *New York*

Class of 1861 Prize

James Dunlop Paxton,   *New York*

Freshman Honors

William Andrew Robinson,[1] *Pennsylvania*, }
Thomas Daniel Warren, *New York*,   } *Equal*, First Honor

1879

Senior Honors[2]

Special Honors

John D Davis, *Pennsylvania*,   Latin Salutatory
William Francis Magie, *New Jersey*,   Valedictory Oration
Donald Campbell McLaren, *New Jersey*,   English Salutatory

Special Honorary Orations[3]

Adrian Riker, *New Jersey*,   Latin
Peter Joseph Hamilton, *Alabama*,   Philosophy

---

[1] Robinson and Warren equal in scholarship, average 97 5   *Minutes of the Faculty*, June 14, 1878

[2] "Owing to the addition of a fourth year to the Curriculum, in 1875–'76, the present Senior class in the School of Science has had but one member, who entered the Sophomore class at the date last mentioned, Mr William M Rice." *Ibid*, June 4, 1879

[3] Awarded for special excellence in particular departments   *Ibid*

Fletcher Durell, *New Jersey*,	Mathematics
Chalmers Martin, *New Jersey*,	Ethics
William Royal Wilder, *New Jersey*,	Greek
Robert Randolph Henderson, *Maryland*,	Mental Science
Alfred L Dennis, Jr , *New Jersey*,	Chemistry
John Farr,[1] *New York*,	Modern Languages
William F Stoutenburgh, *New Jersey*,	Philosophy
Cleveland H. Dodge,[2] *New York*,	Physical Science
William Brewster Lee, *New York*,	Political Science
William Earl Dodge, *New York*,	Philosophy
Robert Bridges, *Pennsylvania*,	English Literature

Fellows

Marquand Fellow in Classical Literature

John D. Davis,   *Pennsylvania*

J S K Fellow in Mathematics

Fletcher Durell,   *New Jersey*

Chancellor Green Fellow in Mental Science

Peter Joseph Hamilton,   *Alabama*

Boudinot Fellow in Modern Languages

Everard De Renne,   *Georgia*

Boudinot Fellow in History

Harold Godwin,   *New York*

Prizemen

Class of 1859 Prize in English Literature

Abram Woodruff Halsey,   *New Jersey*

George Potts Bible Prizes

Frank Patrick Gilman,   *New York*
James Luther Leeper,   *Pennsylvania*

---

[1] Farr and Stoutenburgh equal in scholarship, average 94 6   *Minutes of the Faculty*, June 4, 1879

[2] C H Dodge and Lee equal, average 94 4   *Ibid*

Science and Religion Prize

Robert Harris McCarter,	*New Jersey*

Lynde Prize Debate

Cltosophic Society

Abram Woodruff Halsey,	*New Jersey*
Peter Joseph Hamilton,	*Alabama*
Chalmers Martin,	*New Jersey*

American Whig Society

Robert Bridges,	*Pennsylvania*
Matthew Gault Emery, Jr ,	*District of Columbia*
Samuel Allen Harlow,	*New York*

Lynde Debate Prizemen

Abram Woodruff Halsey,	First Prize
Robert Bridges,	Second Prize
Samuel Allen Harlow,	Third Prize

Junior Honors

Henry Burchard Fine, *Minnesota*,	First Honor

Junior Orators

Cltosophic Society

Ellis Walton Hedges,	*New Jersey*
Cæsar Augustus Rodney Janvier,	*India*
William Mitchell Paden,	*Pennsylvania*
Walter Lorenzo Sheldon,	*Vermont*

American Whig Society

Richard Field Conover,	*New Jersey*
James McCafferty Galbreath,	*Pennsylvania*
George S Johns,	*Missouri*
Irving Platt Withington,	*New York*

Junior Orator Medalists

William Mitchell Paden,	First Medal
Irving Platt Withington,	Second Medal
Richard Field Conover,	Third Medal
George S. Johns,	Fourth Medal

PRIZEMEN

Maclean Prize

William Mitchell Paden,	*Pennsylvania*

Dickinson Prize

Arthur Ames Bliss,	*Pennsylvania*

Sophomore Honors

Stinnecke Scholar

William Andrew Robinson,	*Pennsylvania*

Stinnecke Prizemen

Edwin Augustus Dix,	*New Jersey*
William Andrew Robinson,	*Pennsylvania*
Thomas Daniel Warren,	*New York*

Class of 1861 Prize

Arthur Lalanne Kimball,	*New Jersey*

Freshman Honors

George De Forest Lord Day, *New York*,	First Honor

1880

Senior Honors [1]

Special Honors

Henry Burchard Fine, *Minnesota*,	Latin Salutatory
James Dunlop Paxton, *New York*,	English Salutatory

[1] School of Science honormen not announced in the Faculty minutes

Cæsar Augustus Rodney Janvier, *India*,
                    Philosophical and Classical Oration
Richard Field Conover, *New Jersey*,   Valedictory Oration

Special Honorary Orations and Theses

Vernon Murray Olyphant, *New York*,   Classics
James McCafferty Galbreath, *Pennsylvania*,   Mental Science
Howard Bratton, *Maryland*,   Biology
Walter Lorenzo Sheldon, *Vermont*,   Belles Lettres
James William Parkhill, *Illinois*,   Modern Languages
Caspar Robue Gregory, Jr , *Pennsylvania*,   Chemistry
Ellis Walton Hedges, *New Jersey*,   Geology
David Collins Reid, *New York*,   Metaphysics
William James Gibson, *New Jersey*,   Physics
Henry Clay Ewing, *Pennsylvania*,   Chemistry
John Barclay Keenan, *Pennsylvania*,   German
David Meade Massie, *Ohio*,   Political Science
Charles Walter Scribner, *New Jersey*,   Mathematics

FELLOWS

Marquand Fellow in Classical Literature

Cæsar Augustus Rodney Janvier,   *India*

J S K Fellow in Mathematics

Charles Walter Scribner,   *New Jersey*

Chancellor Green Fellow in Mental Science

James Dunlop Paxton,   *New York*

Class of 1860 Fellow in Experimental Science

Henry Burchard Fine,   *Minnesota*

Boudinot Fellow in Modern Languages

Benjamin Sayre Comstock,   *New York*

Boudinot Fellow in History

Henry Fay Greene,   *Maryland*

E M Fellow in Physical Science

Malcolm McNeill, '77,   *Illinois*

E M Fellow in Biological Science

Henry Fairfield Osborn, '77,   *New York*

Prizemen

Class of 1859 Prize in English Literature

William Mitchell Paden,   *Pennsylvania*

George Potts Bible Prize

William Closson McGarvey,   *New Jersey*

Science and Religion Prize

James McCafferty Galbreath,   *Pennsylvania*

Lynde Prize Debate

Clhosophic Society

Michael Dunn,   *New Jersey*
Cæsar Augustus Rodney Janvier,   *India*
William Mitchell Paden,   *Pennsylvania*

American Whig Society

James McCafferty Galbreath,   *Pennsylvania*
Henry Fay Greene,   *Maryland*
James William Parkhill,   *Illinois*

Lynde Debate Prizemen

Cæsar Augustus Rodney Janvier,   First Prize
Henry Fay Greene,   Second Prize
William Mitchell Paden,   Third Prize

Junior Honors

Edwin Augustus Dix, *New Jersey*,   First Honor

Junior Orators
Cliosophic Society

Charles E. Dunn,	*New Jersey*
David Adams Haynes,	*District of Columbia*
Paul Van Dyke,	*New York*
James Marquis Wilson,	*Pennsylvania*

American Whig Society

Richard Davenport Harlan,	*Kentucky*
Joseph Derwin Hubbard,	*Iowa*
Francis Loney,	*Maryland*
Henry McAlpin, Jr.,	*Georgia*

Junior Orator Medalists

Richard Davenport Harlan,	First Medal
Paul Van Dyke,	Second Medal
James Marquis Wilson,	Third Medal
Joseph Derwin Hubbard,	Fourth Medal

Prizemen
Maclean Prize

Richard Davenport Harlan,	*Kentucky*

Dickinson Prize [1]

Edwin Augustus Dix,	*New Jersey*

Stinnecke Scholar

William Andrew Robinson,	*Pennsylvania*

Sophomore Honors

George De Forest Lord Day, *New York*,	First Honor

Stinnecke Prize

George De Forest Lord Day,	*New York*
John Grier Hibben,	*Illinois*
George Yardley Taylor,	*New Jersey*

---

[1] With honorable mention of Charles Edmiston Craven of New Jersey

Class of 1861 Prize

John Grier Hibben,   *Illinois*

Freshman Honors

Henry Mohr Landis, *Pennsylvania*,   First Honor

1881

Senior Honors

Special Honors

Edwin Augustus Dix, *New Jersey*,   Latin Salutatory
Richard Davenport Harlan,[1] *Kentucky*,   Valedictory Oration
William Andrew Robinson, *Pennsylvania*,   English Salutatory

Special Honorary Orations

Arthur Lalanne Kimball, *New Jersey*,   Physical Science
Andrew Campbell Armstrong, Jr , *New York*,   Philosophy
William Schauffler Dodd, *New Jersey*,   Greek
Thomas Daniel Warren, *New York*,   Latin
Charles Carroll Robbins, *New Jersey*,   Mathematics
John Oliver Halsted Pitney, *New Jersey*,   General Excellence
Arthur H Scribner, *New York*,   (*Thesis*) General Excellence
Thomas William Cauldwell,[2] *New York*,   Natural Science
Charles Giant Titsworth, *New Jersey*,   General Excellence
T. H Powers Farr, *New York*,   General Excellence
Paul Van Dyke, *New York*,   English Literature

SCHOOL OF SCIENCE

General Science

Lewis Davidson Ricketts, *New Jersey*,   First Honor

Civil Engineering

George G Townsend, *Maryland*,   First Honor

---

[1] Harlan and Robinson equal in scholarship, average 97 4   *Minutes of the Faculty*, June 4, 1881
[2] Cauldwell and Titsworth equal, average 94   *Ibid*

Fellows

Marquand Fellow in Classical Literature
William Andrew Robinson, *Pennsylvania*

J S K Fellow in Mathematics
Charles Carroll Robbins, *New Jersey*

Chancellor Green Fellow in Mental Science
Andrew Campbell Armstrong, Jr., *New York*

Class of 1860 Fellow in Experimental Science
Arthur Lalanne Kimball, *New Jersey*

Boudinot Fellow in Modern Languages
Theodore B Schneideman, *Pennsylvania*

Boudinot Fellow in History
Edwin Augustus Dix, *New Jersey*

E. M. Fellow in Physical Science
Malcolm McNeill, '77, *Illinois*

E M Fellow in Biological Science
Henry Fairfield Osborn, '77, *New York*

Fellow in Chemistry and Mineralogy
Lewis Davidson Ricketts, *New Jersey*

Prizemen

Class of 1859 Prize in English Literature
Paul Van Dyke, *New York*

George Potts Bible Prizes
Charles Grant Titsworth, *New Jersey*
George Canfield Frost, *Michigan*

Science and Religion Prize
James Steele Hillhouse, *Georgia*

LYNDE PRIZE DEBATE

Cliosophic Society

David Adams Haynes,   *District of Columbia*
James Steele Hillhouse,   *Georgia*
Paul Van Dyke,   *New York*

American Whig Society

Richard Davenport Harlan,   *Kentucky*
Thomas Danforth King,   *Ohio*
David Wills, Jr.,   *Georgia*

Lynde Debate Prizemen

David Adams Haynes,   First Prize
Richard Davenport Harlan,   Second Prize
Paul Van Dyke,   Third Prize

Junior Honors

George De Forest Lord Day, *New York*,   First Honor

JUNIOR ORATORS

Cliosophic Society

William E. Beattie,   *South Carolina*
George Francis Greene,   *New York*
Robert Crawford Hallock,   *Ohio*
James Adam McWilliams,   *New York*

American Whig Society

Alfred Farmer Burt,   *Pennsylvania*
George De Forest Lord Day,   *New York*
John Grier Hibben,   *Illinois*
Thomas Peebles,   *Pennsylvania*

Junior Orator Medalists

James Adam McWilliams,   First Medal
Thomas Peebles,   Second Medal

George De Forest Lord Day,   Third Medal
John Grier Hibben,   Fourth Medal

Prizemen

Maclean Prize
George Francis Greene,   *New York*

Dickinson Prize
Theodore Potter,   *Ohio*

Sophomore Honors

Benjamin Wiestling Mitchell, *Pennsylvania*,   First Honor

Class of 1861 Prize
Henry Mohr Landis,   *Pennsylvania*

Freshman Honors

Robert Kelly Prentice, *New York*,   First Honor

1882

Senior Honors[1]

Special Honors

George De Forest Lord Day, *New York*,   Latin Salutatory
John Grier Hibben, *Illinois*,   Valedictory Oration
George Yardley Taylor, *New Jersey*,   English Salutatory

Special Honorary Orations and Theses

Thomas Peebles, *Pennsylvania*,   Mental Science
Alfred Farmer Burt, *Pennsylvania*,   Philosophy
Edward B Critchlow, *Utah*,   Philosophy
Henry Crew, *Ohio*,   Chemistry
William B Sherwood, *New York*,   General Excellence
Charles Alfred Lindsley, *New Jersey*,   General Excellence
George Peck Pierson, *New Jersey*,   Classics

---

[1] School of Science honormen not announced in the Faculty minutes

George Francis Greene,[1] *New York,*   Belles Lettres
Alfred Elmer Mills, *New Jersey,*   General Excellence
Edward Smallwood Hughes,   *North Carolina*
Paul Martin,   *New Jersey*
Clark H Marshall,   *Pennsylvania*
Charles Van Loon Gabriel,   *Pennsylvania*
Charles Ramey Milford,   *Indiana*
Robert Haldane West, *Pennsylvania,*
                                   Mathematics and Astronomy
William Carey Howell,   *Iowa*
Robert Crawford Hallock,   *Ohio*
Pennington Ranney, *New Jersey,*   Chemistry

FELLOWS

Marquand Fellow in Classical Literature

George Peck Pierson,   *New Jersey*

J S K Fellow in Mathematics

John Grier Hibben,   *Illinois*

Chancellor Green Fellow in Mental Science

Thomas Peebles,   *Pennsylvania*

Class of 1860 Fellow in Experimental Science

Henry Crew,   *Ohio*

Boudinot Fellow in Modern Languages

C Barton Monroe Harris,   *Maryland*

Boudinot Fellow in History

George Francis Greene,   *New York*

E M Fellow in Physical Science

Malcolm McNeill, '77,   *Illinois*

---

[1] Greene and Mills equal in scholarship, average 93 1   *Minutes of the Faculty,* June 16, 1882

E M Fellow in Biological Science

Henry Fairfield Osborn, '77, *New York*

Ward Fellow in Economic Geology

Lewis Davidson Ricketts. '81, *New Jersey*

Prizemen

Class of 1859 Prize in English Literature

Robert Crawford Hallock, *Ohio*

George Potts Bible Prizes

John Jay Ralston, *Pennsylvania*
Lewis R. Scudder, *Connecticut*

Science and Religion Prize

James Adam McWilliams, *New York*

Lynde Prize Debate

Clıosophic Society

Henry Crew, *Ohio*
Lewis R Scudder, *Connecticut*
George Yardley Taylor, *New Jersey*

American Whig Society

Jeremiah Clinton Cromer, *Indiana*
George De Forest Lord Day, *New York*
Thomas Peebles, *Pennsylvania*

Lynde Debate Prizemen

George Yardley Taylor, First Prize
Thomas Peebles, Second Prize
Henry Crew, Third Prize

Baird Prizemen

James Adam McWilliams, *New York,* ⎫
Thomas Peebles, *Pennsylvania,* ⎬ *Equal,* Baird Prize
George De Forest Lord Day, *New York,* ⎭ Oratory

Robert Crawford Hallock, *Ohio*,   Poetry
Henry Crew, *Ohio, First*,
George Francis Greene, *New York, Second*,   Disputation

Junior Honors

Henry Mohr Landis, *Pennsylvania*,   First Honor

Junior Orators

Cliosophic Society

Claude Ross Brodhead,   *New Jersey*
Otto Crouse,   *New Jersey*
Charles Wesley Lynde,   *New Jersey*
Edwin Milton Royle,   *Utah*

American Whig Society

John Aspinwall Hodge, Jr ,   *Connecticut*
John Lawrence Keller,   *New Jersey*
William Church Osborn,   *New York*
William Kinkead Shelby,   *Kentucky*

Junior Orator Medalists

William Kinkead Shelby,   First Medal
John Aspinwall Hodge, Jr.,   Second Medal
Edwin Milton Royle,   Third Medal
Charles Wesley Lynde,   Fourth Medal

Prizemen

Maclean Prize

William Kinkead Shelby,   *Kentucky*

Dickinson Prize

Albert Pruden Carman,   *New Jersey*

Sophomore Honors

Alfred Gandy Reeves, *New Jersey*,   First Honor

Class of 1861 Prize

Alfred Gandy Reeves, *New Jersey*

Freshman Honors

William Brown McIlvaine, *Illinois*, First Honor

1883

Senior Honors[1]

Special Honors

Henry Mohr Landis,[2] *Pennsylvania*, Latin Salutatory
Benjamin Wiestling Mitchell, *Pennsylvania*,
  English Salutatory and Classical Oration
Otto Crouse, *New Jersey*, Valedictory Oration

Special Honorary Orations and Theses

Albert Pruden Carman, *New Jersey*,
  Belles Lettres and Physical Science
Robert Davison Petty, *New Jersey*,
  Modern Languages and Literature
Andrew Wilkins Wilson, Jr., *Pennsylvania*, Political Science
John Andrew Hiestand,[3] *Pennsylvania*, Philosophy and Ethics
Frank Evans Hoskins, *Pennsylvania*, Philosophy
Aaron Condit Ward, *New Jersey*, Natural Science
George Edwards, *Iowa*, General Excellence
George W. Gilmore, *New York*, Classics
Thomas C. Summerill,[4] *New Jersey*, Astronomy and Philosophy
Edward Vollrath, *Ohio*, Philosophy and Physical Science
John Gormley Murdoch, *New Jersey*, Philosophy
Evan Mohr Landis, *Pennsylvania*

---

[1] Senior honormen of the School of Science not announced in the Faculty minutes

[2] Landis and Mitchell equal in scholarship and equally entitled to the first honor, average 98.4 *Minutes of the Faculty*, June 15, 1883.

[3] Hiestand and Hoskins equal, average 95 1. *Ibid*

[4] Summerill and Vollrath equal, average 93.5. *Ibid*

John Crawford Life,   *Pennsylvania*
Samuel McClellan Davis,[1]   *Pennsylvania*
Lucius Allen Lewis,   *Oregon*
Russell Wellman Moore,   *New Jersey*
William Kinkead Shelby,[2] *Kentucky,*   Belles Lettres
Hartley Titus Updike,   *New Jersey*

FELLOWS

Fellow in Classical Literature
Benjamin Wiestling Mitchell,   *Pennsylvania*

J S K Fellow in Mathematics
Henry Mohr Landis,   *Pennsylvania*

Chancellor Green Fellow in Mental Science
John Gormley Murdoch,   *New Jersey*

Class of 1860 Fellow in Experimental Science
Albert Pruden Carman,   *New Jersey*

Boudinot Fellow in Modern Languages
Henry A Towle,   *New Jersey*

Boudinot Fellow in History
John Aspinwall Hodge, Jr ,   *Connecticut*

E M. Fellow in Biological Science
Walter Mead Rankin,[3]   *New Jersey*

Ward Fellow in Economic Electricity
Henry Crew, '82,   *Ohio*

PRIZEMEN

Class of 1859 Prize in English Literature
Thomas Ross Paden,   *Pennsylvania*

---

[1] Davis and Lewis equal in scholarship, average 91 4   *Minutes of the Faculty*, June 15, 1883.

[2] Shelby and Updike equal, average 90 3   *Ibid.*

[3] W M Rankin, A B , of Williams College.

George Potts Bible Prizes

George Edwards,	*Iowa*
William Parker Finney,	*Maryland*
Charles Alexander Richmond,	*New Jersey*

Science and Religion Prize

Claude Ross Brodhead,	*New Jersey*

LYNDE PRIZE DEBATE

Cliosophic Society

Otto Crouse,	*New Jersey*
Robert Davison Petty,	*New Jersey*
Edwin Milton Royle,	*Utah*

American Whig Society

John Aspinwall Hodge, Jr ,	*Connecticut*
John Lawrence Keller,	*New Jersey*
Samuel McClellan Davis,	*Pennsylvania*

Lynde Debate Prizemen

John Aspinwall Hodge, Jr.,	First Prize
Otto Crouse,	Second Prize
Edwin Milton Royle,	Third Prize

BAIRD PRIZEMEN

Edwin Milton Royle, *Utah*,	Baird Prize
John Aspinwall Hodge, Jr , *Connecticut,*	Oratory
John Lawrence Keller, *New Jersey*,	Delivery
Robert S. Yard, *New Jersey*,	Poetry [1]
Otto Crouse, *New Jersey, First,*	Disputation
Robert Davison Petty, *New Jersey, Second,*	

Junior Honors

Alfred Gandy Reeves, *New Jersey*,	First Honor

---

[1] With honorable mention of Frederick Barnard White of New York

Junior Orators
Chosophic Society

James Mark Baldwin,	*South Carolina*
Leonidas Dennis,	*New Jersey*
John Campbell Murray,	*New Jersey*
George Edward Woodhull,	*Wisconsin*

American Whig Society

John Maynard Harlan,	*District of Columbia*
George McLean Harper,	*Pennsylvania*
Ferdinand Jelke, Jr.,	*Ohio*
Starling Lyne Marshall,	*Kentucky*

Junior Orator Medalists

Leonidas Dennis,	First Medal
George McLean Harper,	Second Medal
John Maynard Harlan,	Third Medal
James Mark Baldwin,	Fourth Medal

Prizemen
Maclean Prize

James Mark Baldwin,	*South Carolina*

Dickinson Prize

John Newton Forman,	*India*

Sophomore Honors

William Brown McIlvaine, *Illinois*,	First Honor

Class of 1861 Prize

William Brown McIlvaine,	*Illinois*

Freshman Honors

Matthew Corry Fleming, *Ohio*,	First Honor

1884

Senior Honors[1]

Special Honors

Alfred Gandy Reeves, *New Jersey*,	Latin Salutatory
James Mark Baldwin, *South Carolina*,	Valedictory Oration
Henry Bell Gayley,[2] *Maryland*,	
	Philosophical and Classical Oration
Robert Kelly Prentice, *New York*,	English Salutatory

Special Honorary Orations and Theses

Angier Bailey Hobbs, *District of Columbia*,	Ethics
Alexander Horton Travis, *New York*,	Astronomy
George Prentiss Butler,[3] *New York*,	Philosophy
Thomas McBride Nichols, *Pennsylvania*,	General Excellence
Henry Neill Paul, *Pennsylvania*,	General Excellence
Albert Matthews Jackson,	*Pennsylvania*
Charles Tabele MacMullin,	*Ohio*
William Marvin Langdon,[4]	*New York*
Alvin Fayette Lewis, *Kentucky*,	Philosophy
Thomas Joseph McCormick,	*New York*
William Chester,	*District of Columbia*
Charles Sumner Hamilton, *Ohio*,	Greek
John Howard Neely,	*Pennsylvania*
Alvin Blackwell,	*New Jersey*
Ambrose Giddings Todd,	*New Jersey*
Robert Fulton McMahon, *Ohio*,	Political Philosophy
Alexander Spencer Rowland, *New Jersey*,	Physics

George McLean Harper,[5] *Pennsylvania*,	English Literature

[1] School of Science honormen not announced

[2] Gayley and Prentice equal in scholarship, average 97 8   *Minutes of the Faculty*, June 13, 1884

[3] Butler and Nichols equal, average 95 9   *Ibid*

[4] Langdon and Lewis equal, average 94 1   *Ibid*

[5] Harper's average was 88 9   *Ibid*

FELLOWS

Fellow in Classical Literature

Henry Bell Gayley,   *Maryland*

J. S. K Fellow in Mathematics

Alfred Gandy Reeves,   *New Jersey*

Chancellor Green Fellow in Mental Science

James Mark Baldwin,   *South Carolina*

Class of 1860 Fellow in Experimental Science

Alexander Spencer Rowland,   *New Jersey*

Boudinot Fellow in Modern Languages

John Campbell Murray,   *New Jersey*

Boudinot Fellow in History

Thomas Joseph McCormick,   *New York*

E M Fellow in Biological Science

John Ellsworth Peters, '70,   *New Jersey*

PRIZEMEN

Class of 1859 Prize in English Literature

George McLean Harper,   *Pennsylvania*

George Potts Bible Prizes

William Marvin Langdon,   *New York*
Robert Woods Van Kirk,   *Pennsylvania*

Science and Religion Prize

William Chester,   *District of Columbia*

LYNDE PRIZE DEBATE

Cliosophic Society

James Mark Baldwin,   *South Carolina*
Eugene Miller,   *Kentucky*
Robert Kelly Prentice,   *New York*

American Whig Society

John Maynard Harlan,	*District of Columbia*
Alfred Gandy Reeves,	*New Jersey*
Claude Milton Thomas,	*Kentucky*

Lynde Debate Prizemen

Robert Kelly Prentice,	First Prize
Claude Milton Thomas,	Second Prize
John Maynard Harlan,	Third Prize

BAIRD PRIZEMEN

James Mark Baldwin, *South Carolina*,	Baird Prize
Job Elmer Hedges, *New York*,	Oratory
George McLean Harper, *Pennsylvania*,	Delivery
Thomas McBride Nichols, *Pennsylvania*,	Poetry
John Campbell Murray, *New Jersey, First*,	Disputation
Alfred Gandy Reeves, *New Jersey, Second*,	

Junior Honors

William Brown McIlvaine, *Illinois*,	First Honor

JUNIOR ORATORS

Clfosophic Society

Duncan Edwards,	*New York*
Samuel Harper Leeper, Jr,	*Pennsylvania*
Clarence Walworth McIlvaine,	*Vermont*
Robert Parmelee Wilder,	*India*

American Whig Society

Grant Robinson Bennett,	*Wisconsin*
James Harlan Cleveland,	*Kentucky*
William Waddell Conner,	*Iowa*
John Kimberly Mumford,	*New York*

Junior Orator Medalists

Grant Robinson Bennett,	First Medal
Duncan Edwards,	Second Medal
Robert Parmelee Wilder,	Third Medal
Samuel Harper Leeper, Jr.,	Fourth Medal

PRIZEMEN

Maclean Prize

Clarence Walworth McIlvaine,	*Vermont*

Dickinson Prize

Frank Stiles Woodruff,	*New Jersey*

Sophomore Honors

Matthew Corry Fleming, *Ohio*,	First Honor

Class of 1861 Prize

George Black Roddy,	*Pennsylvania*

Freshman Honors

William Hallock Johnson, *New York*,	First Honor

1885

Senior Honors[1]

Special Honors

William Brown McIlvaine, *Illinois*,	Latin Salutatory
Clarence Walworth McIlvaine, *Vermont*,	Valedictory Oration
James Wilson Bayard, *Pennsylvania*,	English Salutatory
James Harlan Cleveland, *Kentucky*,	Philosophical Oration

Special Honorary Orations and Theses

Jonathan Sturges, *New York*,	English Literature
George Britton Durell, *New Jersey*,	Experimental Science

[1] School of Science honormen not announced

Max Brunswick Nahm, *Kentucky,*   Political Science
John Edgar Johnson, Jr , *New York,*   Chemistry
Sanford Norris Knapp, *New York,*   Astronomy
Charles Flint McClumpha, *New York,*   Philosophy
Sherrerd Depue, *New Jersey,*   Constitutional Law
Robert Eber Carter, *New Yoi k,*   Biology
Reuben S Lawrence, *Kansas,*   General Excellence
Henry Dallas Thompson, *California,*   Mathematics
Robert Hezekiah Beattie,[1] *New York,*   Mental Science
James Edward Hayes, *New Jersey,*   Metaphysics
Frank Stiles Woodruff, *New Jersey,*   General Excellence

FELLOWS

Fellow in Classical Literature

Monroe Crawford,   *New Jersey*

J S K. Fellow in Mathematics

Henry Dallas Thompson,   *California*

Chancellor Green Fellow in Mental Science

James Harlan Cleveland,   *Kentucky*

Class of 1860 Fellow in Experimental Science

George Britton Durell,   *New Jersey*

Boudinot Fellow in Modern Languages

Paul Adrian Scharff,   *New Jersey*

Boudinot Fellow in History

James Wilson Bayard,   *Pennsylvania*

E M Fellow in Biological Science

Robert Eber Carter,   *New York*

PRIZEMEN

Class of 1859 Prize in English Literature

Clarence Walworth McIlvaine,   *Vermont*

---

[1] Beattie and Hayes equal in scholarship, average 92 8   *Minutes of the Faculty,* June 3, 1885

George Potts Bible Prizes

Reuben S Lawrence,	*Kansas*
John Crary Lord,	*New Jersey*
William Henry Robinson,	*New York*

Science and Religion Prize

Frank Stiles Woodruff,	*New Jersey*

Atwater Prize in Political Science

Sherrerd Depue,	*New Jersey*

Lynde Prize Debate

Chosophic Society

Sherrerd Depue,	*New Jersey*
Charles Flint McClumpha,	*New York*
Clarence Walworth McIlvaine,	*Vermont*

American Whig Society

James Harlan Cleveland,	*Kentucky*
Monroe Crawford,	*New Jersey*
Edmund Wilson,	*New Jersey*

Lynde Debate Prizemen

Edmund Wilson,	First Prize
Sherrerd Depue,	Second Prize
Monroe Crawford,	Third Prize

Baird Prizemen

Charles Flint McClumpha, *New York*,	Baird Prize
James Harlan Cleveland, *Kentucky*,	Oratory
William Henry Robinson, *New York*,	Delivery
Frank Stiles Woodruff, *New Jersey*,	Poetry
Sherrerd Depue, *New Jersey, First*, James Wilson Bayard, *Pennsylvania, Second.*	Disputation

Junior Honors

George Black Roddy, *Pennsylvania*,	First Honor

JUNIOR ORATORS

Cliosophic Society

Anthony Woodward Durell,	*New Jersey*
George A Tryon Eddy,	*New York*
Wilson Farrand,	*New Jersey*
William Rankin,	*New Jersey*

American Whig Society

Charles Rosenbury Erdman,	*New York*
John W. Harding,	*Pennsylvania*
William Jessup,	*Pennsylvania*
Marion Mills Miller,	*Ohio*

Junior Orator Medalists

Charles Rosenbury Erdman,	First Medal
Marion Mills Miller,	Second Medal
William Jessup,	Third Medal
William Rankin,	Fourth Medal

PRIZEMEN

Maclean Prize

Marion Mills Miller,	*Ohio*

Dickinson Prize[1]

Edward Demoss Miller,	*West Virginia*

Sophomore Honors

William Hallock Johnson, *New York*,	First Honor

Class of 1861 Prize[2]

Samuel Thompson Dodd,	*New York*

Freshman Honors

Winthrop More Daniels, *Ohio*,	First Honor

---

[1] Arnold Guyot Cameron of New Jersey, honorable mention
[2] Francis Ellison Reid of Ohio, honorable mention

1886

Senior Honors[1]

First Group   *Magna cum laude*

George A Tryon Eddy, *New York*,	Valedictory Oration
Matthew Corry Fleming, *Ohio*,	Latin Salutatory
George Black Roddy, *Pennsylvania*,	English Salutatory
Ralph Crowley Sheldon, *New York*,	Political Science Oration

Special Honors   *Cum laude*

Joseph Deyoe Baucus, *New York*, American Constitutional Law
James Harrington Boyd, *Ohio*, Mathematics
Arnold Guyot Cameron, *New Jersey*,
      English Literature and Greek
John Watson Cary, Jr., *Wisconsin*, American Political History
Harry Charles Elsing, *Illinois*, Continental Literature
Charles Rosenbury Erdman, *New York*, Philosophy
Frederick Evans, Jr , *Pennsylvania*, General Excellence
Walter Lowrie Hervey, *Ohio*, Political Economy
John Cass Mathis, *Illinois*, History
Edward Demoss Miller, *West Virginia*, Ethics
Marion Mills Miller, *Ohio*, Belles Lettres
Taylor Reed, *Pennsylvania*, Physics
John Archer Silver, *Maryland*, Modern Languages
Oliver Smith Strong, *New Jersey*, Metaphysics
Robert Parmelee Wilder, *India*, Mental Science

Wilson Farrand,[2]   *New Jersey*

[1] Hereafter the arrangement of Senior honors will include the First Group, and such members of other groups as shall have attained special honors as indicated. The First Group, *magna cum laude*, indicates "very high standing," and includes those students whose general average does not exceed 1.3. The names are alphabetically arranged under each head *Minutes of the Faculty*, June 11, 1886

[2] "Entitled to a place in the Honor List, but had not been regularly examined on account of ill-health " *Ibid*, June 7, 1886

Fellows

Fellow in Classical Literature
George Black Roddy,   *Pennsylvania*

J. S. K. Fellow in Mathematics
James Harrington Boyd,   *Ohio*

Chancellor Green Fellow in Mental Science
Edward Demoss Miller,   *West Virginia*

Class of 1860 Fellow in Experimental Science
Taylor Reed,   *Pennsylvania*

Boudinot Fellow in Modern Languages
Harry Charles Elsing,   *Illinois*

Boudinot Fellow in History
John Cass Mathis,   *Illinois*

E. M. Fellow in Biological Science
John Warne Phillips, '84,   *New Jersey*

Prizemen

Class of 1859 Prize in English Literature
Arnold Guyot Cameron,   *New Jersey*

Alexander Guthrie McCosh Prize
George A. Tryon Eddy,   *New York*

George Potts Bible Prizes
John Archer Silver,   *Maryland*
Robert Parmelee Wilder,   *India*

Science and Religion Prize
Charles Helliwell,   *New Jersey*

Atwater Prize in Political Science
Francis Fisher Kane,   *Pennsylvania*

Lynde Prize Debate

Cliosophic Society

William Simpson Elder	*Ohio*
Wilson Farrand,	*New Jersey*
John Cass Mathis,	*Illinois*

American Whig Society

Joseph Deyoe Baucus,	*New York*
Richard Morse Hodge,	*Connecticut*
Henry Winans Jessup,	*Pennsylvania*

Lynde Debate Prizemen

Wilson Farrand,	First Prize
Richard Morse Hodge,	Second Prize
Henry Winans Jessup,	Third Prize

Baird Prizemen

George A. Tryon Eddy, *New York*,	Baird Prize
Walter Lowrie Hervey, *Ohio*, ⎱ *Equal*, Robert Parmelee Wilder, *India*, ⎰	Oratory
Marion Mills Miller, *Ohio*,	Delivery
Marion Mills Miller, *Ohio*,	Poetry
Anthony Woodward Durell, *New Jersey, First*, Ralph Crowley Sheldon, *New York, Second*,	Disputation

Junior Honors

Roger Bruce Cash Johnson, *West Indies*,	First Honor

Junior Orators

Cliosophic Society

George Titus Berry,	*New Jersey*
Roger Bruce Cash Johnson,	*West Indies*
John Wahl Queen, Jr ,	*New Jersey*
George Livingstone Robinson,	*New York*

American Whig Society

Robert William Mason,	*Ohio*
Paul Clement Matthews,	*District of Columbia*
Peter McHarg McQueen,	*Scotland*
Frank Hyatt Smith,	*Michigan*

Junior Orator Medalists

Robert William Mason,	First Medal
Frank Hyatt Smith,	Second Medal
George Livingstone Robinson,	Third Medal
Paul Clement Matthews,	Fourth Medal

PRIZEMEN

Maclean Prize

Roger Bruce Cash Johnson,   *West Indies*

Dickinson Prize

Francis Harding White,   *District of Columbia*

Sophomore Honors

Class of 1861 Prize

Edwin Mortimer Hopkins,   *New York*

Freshman Honors

Fred Neher, *New York*,   First Honor

1887

Senior Honors

FIRST GROUP *Magna cum laude*

Roger Bruce Cash Johnson, *West Indies*,   Latin Salutatory

SPECIAL HONORS *Cum laude*

Robert William Blake, *New Jersey*,	Greek
Wilmot Albert Carrington, *District of Columbia*,	International Law
Solomon Stanger Iszard, *New Jersey*,	General Excellence

Charles Hill Macloskie, *New Jersey*,   General Excellence
Paul Clement Matthews, *District of Columbia*, Valedictory Oration
Peter McHarg McQueen, *Scotland*,   Metaphysics
James Paige, *Minnesota*,   Political Economy
Francis Ellison Reid, *Ohio*,   English Salutatory
Clarence William Rouse, *New York*,   Classics
Alfred Hedges Scofield, *New Jersey*,   Physical Science
Frank Hyatt Smith, *Michigan*,   History
Lucien Waggener, Jr , *Kentucky*,   Modern Languages

Samuel Thompson Dodd, *New York*,   Mathematics
George Livingstone Robinson, *New York*,   General Excellence
Francis Harding White, *District of Columbia*,   Political Science

Fellows

Fellow in Classical Literature

Robert William Blake,   *New Jersey*

J S K Fellow in Mathematics[1]

Samuel Thompson Dodd,   *New York*

Chancellor Green Fellow in Mental Science

Roger Bruce Cash Johnson,   *West Indies*

Class of 1860 Fellow in Experimental Science

Alfred Hedges Scofield,   *New Jersey*

Boudinot Fellow in Modern Languages

Albert Lincoln Mershon,   *New Jersey*

Boudinot Fellow in History

Francis Harding White,   *District of Columbia*

E M Fellow in Biological Science

Oliver Smith Strong, '86,   *New Jersey*

Class of 1877 University Fellow in Biology

Henry Orr,

---

[1] With the honorable mention of Francis Ellison Reid of Ohio

University Fellow in English
Marion Mills Miller, '86, *Ohio*

South East Club University Fellow in Social Science
John Wahl Queen, Jr., *New Jersey*

PRIZEMEN [1]

Class of 1859 Prize in English Literature
Frank Hyatt Smith, *Michigan*

Alexander Guthrie McCosh Prize
Edward Demoss Miller,[2] *West Virginia*

George Potts Bible Prizes
Wilmot Albert Carrington, *District of Columbia*
George Livingstone Robinson, *New York*

Atwater Prize in Political Science
John Martin Jamison, *Pennsylvania*

LYNDE PRIZE DEBATE

Cliosophic Society
Samuel Thompson Dodd, *New York*
John Wahl Queen, Jr , *New Jersey*
Francis Harding White, *District of Columbia*

American Whig Society
James Walter Doughty, *Ohio*
Frank Hyatt Smith, *Michigan*
Franklin Spencer Spalding, *Colorado*

Lynde Debate Prizemen
Franklin Spencer Spalding, First Prize
Francis Harding White, Second Prize
John Wahl Queen, Jr., Third Prize

---

[1] No award of Science and Religion Prize.
[2] Of the class of 1886

BAIRD PRIZEMEN

Robert William Mason, *Ohio*,	Baird Prize
Paul Clement Matthews, *District of Columbia*,	Oratory
Peter McHarg McQueen, *Scotland*,	Delivery
Mark Harvey Liddell, *Pennsylvania*,	Poetry
James Paige, *Minnesota, First*,	
Samuel Thompson Dodd, *New York, Second*,	Disputation

Junior Honors

Edwin Mortimer Hopkins, *New York*,	First Honor

JUNIOR ORATORS

Closophic Society

Livingston Farrand,	*New Jersey*
Benjamin Van Dyke Hedges,	*New Jersey*
Andrew Harold Miller,	*Pennsylvania*
Walter Augustus Wyckoff,	*India*

American Whig Society

Winthrop More Daniels,	*Ohio*
Charles James Hatfield,	*Pennsylvania*
William Mann Irvine,	*Pennsylvania*
James Hammond Pershing,	*Pennsylvania*

Junior Orator Medalists

James Hammond Pershing,	First Medal
Charles James Hatfield,	Second Medal
Andrew Harold Miller,	Third Medal
Walter Augustus Wyckoff,	Fourth Medal

PRIZEMEN [1]

Maclean Prize

Walter Augustus Wyckoff,	*India*

[1] Dickinson Prize not awarded.

Sophomore Honors
Class of 1861 Prize[1]
John Milton Putnam Brooks,   *Ohio*

Freshman Honors
Edward Phillips Burgess, Jr , *Massachusetts*,   First Honor

1888
Senior Honors

FIRST GROUP *Magna cum laude*

Winthrop More Daniels, *Ohio*,	Valedictory Oration
Hugh Trowbridge Dobbins, *California*,	Latin Salutatory
Edwin Mortimer Hopkins, *New York*,	English Salutatory

SPECIAL HONORS *Cum laude*

Ernest Trow Carter, *New Jersey*,	Philosophy
Russell Carter, *New Jersey*,	General Excellence
Frederick L Drummond, *New Jersey*,	Political Science
William Holmes Forsyth, *New Jersey*,	Modern Languages
William Fryling, *New Jersey*,	Philosophy
Kemper Fullerton, *District of Columbia*,	Classics
William Hallock Johnson, *New York*,	Mental Science
Thomas Marc Parrott, *Ohio*,	English Literature
Peter Rioseco, *Pennsylvania*,	General Excellence
William Henry Runyon, *New Jersey*,	Physical Science
Charles Sidney Smith, *District of Columbia*,	Classics
William Wisner White, *New Jersey*,	General Excellence

FELLOWS

Fellow in Classical Literature
Hugh Trowbridge Dobbins,   *California*

J S K Fellow in Mathematics
Edwin Mortimer Hopkins,   *New York*

[1] With honorable mention of Henry Gurnee Drummond of New Jersey.

Chancellor Green Fellow in Mental Science

William Hallock Johnson,   *New York*

Class of 1860 Fellow in Experimental Science

William Henry Runyon,   *New Jersey*

Boudinot Fellow in Modern Languages

Elliott Verne Richardson,   *New Jersey*

Boudinot Fellow in History

Frederick L. Drummond,   *New Jersey*

E M Fellow in Biological Science

Charles Freeman Williams McClure,   *Massachusetts*

Class of 1877 University Fellow in Biology

Arthur McQuiston Miller, '84,   *Ohio*

University Fellow in English

Mark Harvey Liddell, '87,   *Pennsylvania*

South East Club University Fellow in Social Science

William Mann Irvine,   *Pennsylvania*

University Fellow in Archæology

George B. Hussey,[1]   *New Jersey*

Fellow in Mathematics and Physical Science

Samuel Thompson Dodd,[2] '87,   *New York*

PRIZEMEN

Class of 1859 Prize in English Literature [3]

Thomas Marc Parrott,   *Ohio*

Alexander Guthrie McCosh Prize

Roger Bruce Cash Johnson,[4]   *West Indies*

---

[1] Ph.D , Johns Hopkins University

[2] By courtesy.—*Annual Catalogue, 1888–'89.*

[3] With honorable mention of Peter Rioseco of Pennsylvania

[4] Of the class of 1887

George Potts Bible Prizes

Robert Hutchinson Kirk,	*Pennsylvania*
Charles Alvin Smith,	*Pennsylvania*

Atwater Prize in Political Science

Ralph Earl Prime, Jr.,	*New York*

LYNDE PRIZE DEBATE

Cliosophic Society

Frederick Griswold Beebe,	*New York*
Frederick L Drummond,	*New Jersey*
George Elmer Scott,	*New York*

American Whig Society

Winthrop More Daniels,	*Ohio*
Samuel Colgate Hodge	*Connecticut*
James Hammond Pershing,	*Pennsylvania*

Lynde Debate Prizemen

Winthrop More Daniels,	First Prize
Frederick L. Drummond.	Second Prize
James Hammond Pershing,	Third Prize

BAIRD PRIZEMEN

James Hammond Pershing, *Pennsylvania.*	Baird Prize
Russell Carter. *New Jersey*,	Oratory
Kemper Fullerton, *District of Columbia*,	Delivery
Thomas Marc Parrott, *Ohio*,	Poetry
Samuel Colgate Hodge, *Connecticut*, *First*,	Disputation
Frederick Jay Knox, *New Jersey*, *Second*,	

Junior Honors

Robert Eliot Speer, *Pennsylvania*,	First Honor

Junior Orators
Cliosophic Society

Henry Gurnee Drummond,	*New Jersey*
William James George,	*Ohio*
Robert Eliot Speer,	*Pennsylvania*
David Ripley Todd,	*Kansas*

American Whig Society

William Sabin Chase,	*Ohio*
Thomas W Hotchkiss, Jr ,	*New York*
Robert Henry Life,	*New York*
Clarence Blair Mitchell,	*New Jersey*

Junior Orator Medalists

Robert Eliot Speer,	First Medal
David Ripley Todd,	Second Medal
Henry Gurnee Drummond,	Third Medal
Thomas W Hotchkiss, Jr ,	Fourth Medal

Prizemen [1]
Maclean Prize

Henry Gurnee Drummond,	*New Jersey*

Sophomore Honors
Class of 1861 Prize

John Morris Yeakle,	*Pennsylvania*

Francis Biddle Prize

William Sanderson Furst,	*Pennsylvania*

Freshman Honors

Samuel Grant Oliphant, *New Jersey*,	First Honor

---

[1] No award of the Dickinson Prize

1889

Senior Honors

FIRST GROUP *Magna cum laude*

Lewis Seymour Mudge, *New Jersey*,	Latin Salutatory
Fred Neher, *New York*,	English Salutatory
Robert Eliot Speer, *Pennsylvania*,	Valedictory Oration

SPECIAL HONORS *Cum laude*

Richmond Ogston Aulick, *District of Columbia*,	Political Science
David Bovaird, Jr , *Pennsylvania*,	Chemistry
John Milton Putnam Brooks, *Ohio*,	Mathematics
Henry Gurnee Drummond, *New Jersey*,	Physics
Robert Henry Life, *New York*,	Philosophy
Edmund Yard Robbins, *New Jersey*,	Classics
James Frederick Stebbins, *New York*,	Belles Lettres
Howard Crosby Warren, *New Jersey*,	Mental Science

FELLOWS

Fellow in Classical Literature

Edmund Yard Robbins,	*New Jersey*

J. S. K. Fellow in Mathematics

John Milton Putnam Brooks,	*Ohio*

Chancellor Green Fellow in Mental Science

Howard Crosby Warren,	*New Jersey*

Class of 1860 Fellow in Experimental Science

Lewis Seymour Mudge,	*New Jersey*

Boudinot Fellow in Modern Languages

Joshua Brush Gesner,	*New Jersey*

Boudinot Fellow in History

Henry Gurnee Drummond,	*New Jersey*

L M Fellow in Biological Science

Bertram Howard Waters,   *Pennsylvania*

Class of 1877 University Fellow in Biology

Oliver Smith Strong, '86,   *New Jersey*

University Fellow in English

William Rankin, '86,   *New Jersey*

South East Club University Fellow in Social Science

Richmond Ogston Aulick,   *District of Columbia*

University Fellow in Archæology

George B. Hussey,   *New Jersey*

Special Fellow in Biology

Henry Russell Pemberton,   *Virginia*

PRIZEMEN [1]

Class of 1859 Prize in English Literature

Sidney Dale Furst,   *Pennsylvania*

George Potts Bible Prizes

Andrew Banks,   *Pennsylvania*
Malbone Watson Graham,   *Iowa*

Atwater Prize in Political Science

James Frederick Stebbins,   *New York*

Frederick Barnard White Prize in Architecture

Edward Ringwood Hewitt,   *New York*

Theodore Cuyler Prize in Economics

Gormly J Sproull,   *New York*

LYNDE PRIZE DEBATE

Cliosophic Society

Frank Snowden Katzenbach, Jr.,   *New Jersey*
Robert Eliot Speer,   *Pennsylvania*
David Ripley Todd,   *Kansas*

[1] No award of the Alexander Guthrie McCosh Prize

American Whig Society

Maitland Alexander,	*New York*
Robert Henry Life,	*New York*
Clarence Blair Mitchell,	*New Jersey*

Lynde Debate Prizemen

Robert Eliot Speer,	First Prize
Clarence Blair Mitchell,	Second Prize
David Ripley Todd,	Third Prize

BAIRD PRIZEMEN

Robert Eliot Speer, *Pennsylvania,*	Baird Prize
Robert Henry Life, *New York, and*	Oratory
Thomas Henry Powers Sailer, *Pennsylvania,*	
Maitland Alexander, *New York,*	Delivery
William Laing Merrill, *New York,*	Poetry
Frank Snowden Katzenbach, Jr , *New Jersey, First,*	Disputation
Edmund Yard Robbins, *New Jersey, Second,*	

Junior Honors

Edward Phillips Burgess, Jr., *Massachusetts,*	First Honor

JUNIOR ORATORS

Cliosophic Society

Tileston Fracker Chambers,	*District of Columbia*
Huntington Wolcott Merchant,	*New York*
Clarke Benedict Williams,	*New York*
John Morris Yeakle,	*Pennsylvania*

American Whig Society

Knowlton Lyman Ames,	*Illinois*
Edgworth Bird Baxter,	*Georgia*
James Jeffries Charlton,	*Oregon*
Francis Palmer,	*Maine*

Junior Orator Medalists

Francis Palmer,	First Medal
Edgworth Bird Baxter,	Second Medal
Clarke Benedict Williams,	Third Medal
Knowlton Lyman Ames,	Fourth Medal

PRIZEMEN [1]

Maclean Prize

Edgworth Bird Baxter,   *Georgia*

Sophomore Honors

Class of 1861 Prize [2]

Daniel Warren Poor, Jr,   *Pennsylvania*

Francis Biddle Prize

Samuel Grant Oliphant,   *New Jersey*

Freshman Honors

John Glover Wilson, *Maryland*,   First Honor

1890

Senior Honors

FIRST GROUP   *Magna cum laude*

Edward Phillips Burgess, Jr, *Massachusetts*,   Latin Salutatory
Robert Porter Shick, *Pennsylvania*,   English Salutatory
John Morris Yeakle,   *Pennsylvania*

———

Francis Palmer,[3] *Maine*,   Valedictory Oration

---

[1] Dickinson Prize not awarded

[2] With honorable mention of Cornelius Rea Agnew of New York, and James Henry Dunham of New Jersey.

[3] Of the Second Group, *cum laude*

Special Honors

MENTAL SCIENCE—Edgworth Bird Baxter, *Georgia;* George McFarlane Galt, *Illinois,* Richard Irvin, Jr , *New York*

POLITICAL SCIENCE AND HISTORY—Jacob Benner Hillegass, *Pennsylvania,* Robert Thompson Miller McCready, *Pennsylvania,* Charles Albert Woods, *Pennsylvania,* John Morris Yeakle, *Pennsylvania.*

GREEK AND LATIN — Joseph Reynolds Kerr, Jr., *New York,* Dunlop Moore, Jr., *Pennsylvania,* Robert Porter Shick, *Pennsylvania,* Morris Crater Sutphen, *New Jersey*

FRENCH AND GERMAN—Frederick Morton Wall, *New York*

ENGLISH—Benjamin Haywood Adams, *New Jersey,* Ernest Ludlow Bogart, *New York*

MATHEMATICS AND MATHEMATICAL SCIENCE— John Paul Conduit, *New Jersey,* George Bishop Covington, *Maryland,* Charles Hodge, *Pennsylvania,* Malcolm McLaren, *New York;* George Louis Shearer, *California,* Clarke Benedict Williams, *New York.*

NATURAL SCIENCES — David Linn Edsall, *New Jersey,* James Ditmars Voorhees, *New Jersey.*

FELLOWS

Fellow in Classsical Literature

Robert Porter Shick,   *Pennsylvania*

J S K Fellow in Mathematics

Clarke Benedict Williams,   *New York*

Chancellor Green Fellow in Mental Science

Edgworth Bird Baxter,[1]   *Georgia*

Class of 1860 Fellow in Experimental Science

George Louis Shearer,   *California*

Boudinot Fellow in Modern Languages

Louis Eugene Livingood,   *Pennsylvania*

[1] Resigned.

Boudinot Fellow in History

William Dwight Gibby,   *New Jersey*

E M Fellow in Biological Science

William Cowper Prime,   *New York*

Class of 1877 University Fellow in Biology

Henry Russell Pemberton, '89,   *Virginia*

South East Club University Fellow in Social Science

John Wahl Queen, Jr., '87,   *New Jersey*

University Fellow in Archaeology

George B. Hussey,[1]   *New Jersey*

PRIZEMEN[2]

Class of 1859 Prize in English Literature[3]

William Sanderson Furst,   *Pennsylvania*

Alexander Guthrie McCosh Prizes

Edgworth Bird Baxter, *Georgia*,   First
Frank Lukens, *New Jersey*,   Second

Atwater Prize in Political Science

Joseph William Lewis, Jr.,   *Missouri*

Theodore Cuyler Prize in Economics

George Bishop Covington,   *Maryland*

LYNDE PRIZE DEBATE

Cliosophic Society

Herbert Mortimer Gesner,   *New Jersey*
Huntington Wolcott Merchant,   *New York*
John Morris Yeakle,   *Pennsylvania*

[1] Resigned.

[2] George Potts Bible Prizes not awarded

[3] With honorable mention of Harlie Wallace Hathaway of New Jersey

American Whig Society

James Jeffries Charlton,	*Oregon*
Henry Kreider Denlinger,	*Pennsylvania*
Edmund Grindall Rawson, Jr ,	*New York*

Lynde Debate Prizemen

James Jeffries Charlton,	First Prize
John Morris Yeakle,	Second Prize
Edmund Grindall Rawson, Jr ,	Third Prize

Baird Prizemen

Edgworth Bird Baxter, *Georgia,*	Baird Prize
Francis Palmer, *Maine,*	Oratory
Walter Lowrie, *Pennsylvania,*	Delivery
Hailie Wallace Hathaway, *New Jersey,*	Poetry
Robert Thompson Miller McCready, *Pennsylvania, First,*	
Henry Kreider Denlinger, *Pennsylvania, Second,*	Disputation

Junior Honors

Samuel Grant Oliphant, *New Jersey,*	First Honor

Junior Orators
Cliosophic Society

Edward Waterman Evans, Jr.,	*New Jersey*
Mushegh Minas Minassian,	*Turkey*
Samuel Semple,	*Pennsylvania*
George Herbert Stephens,	*Pennsylvania*

American Whig Society

Pringle Carlisle Jones,	*Ohio*
James Cowden Meyers,	*Pennsylvania*
George Jacobs Parker,	*Pennsylvania*
George Riddle Wallace	*Pennsylvania*

Junior Orator Medalists

George Riddle Wallace,	First Medal
George Jacob Parker,	Second Medal
Pringle Carlisle Jones,	Third Medal
Samuel Semple,	Fourth Medal

PRIZEMEN

Maclean Prize

George Riddle Wallace,   *Pennsylvania*

Dickinson Prize [1]

George Herbert Stephens,   *Pennsylvania*

Frederick Barnard White Prize in Architecture

George Herbert Stephens,   *Pennsylvania*

Mathematical Prizes

John Preston Hoskins, *Pennsylvania*,	First
Clarence McCheyne Gordon, *Pennsylvania*,	Second
Robert Stuart Stewart, *Michigan*,	Third

Thomas B Wanamaker English Prize

Samuel Grant Oliphant,   *New Jersey*

Alexander Guthrie McCosh Prize

Edward Waterman Evans, Jr.,   *New Jersey*

Sophomore Honors

Class of 1861 Prize

Walter Livingston Wright, Jr.,   *New Jersey*

Francis Biddle Prize

Caspar Wistar Hodge, Jr ,   *New Jersey*

Class of 1876 Prize for Debate in Political Economy

Bowdre Phinizy,   *Georgia*

---

[1] With honorable mention of Daniel Warren Poor, Jr , of Pennsylvania.

Freshman Honors

Coitlandt Van Rensselaer Hodge, *New Jersey,*   First Honor

Stinnecke Scholai

Jesse Benedict Cartei,   *New York*

ENTRANCE EXAMINATION PRIZES

Alumni Prize in New Yoik City

Benjamin Brandreth McAlpin,   *New York*

George W Childs Prize in Philadelphia

Horace Lyman Brown Henderson,   *Pennsylvania*
James Slocum Rogeis,   *Pennsylvania*

1891

Senior Honors

FIRST GROUP *Magna cum laude*

James Henry Dunham, *New Jersey,*   English Salutatory
Edward Waterman Evans, Jr ,   *New Jersey*
John Preston Hoskins,   *Pennsylvania*
Glenn Ford McKinney,   *Pennsylvania*
James Cowden Meyers,   *Pennsylvania*
Samuel Grant Oliphant, *New Jersey,*   Latin Salutatory
George Riddle Wallace, *Pennsylvania,*   Valedictory Oration
Charles Dunning White,   *New Jersey*

Special Honors

CLASSICS—Samuel Grant Oliphant, *New Jeisey.*

MATHEMATICS AND MATHEMATICAL SCIENCE—Charles Renwick Campbell, *Pennsylvania,* Clarence McCheyne Gordon, *Pennsylvania,* John Cutler Shedd, *Persia,* Robert Stuart Stewart, *Michigan*

FRENCH AND GERMAN — John Preston Hoskins, *Pennsylvania*

PHILOSOPHY — Wilson Aull, *Missouri,* Edward Waterman Evans, Jr., *New Jersey,* George Herbert Stephens, *Pennsylvania,* Ambrose White Vernon, *New Jersey*

POLITICAL SCIENCE — James Henry Dunham, *New Jersey;* Erskine Hewitt, *New York,* James Cowden Meyers, *Pennsylvania,* George Riddle Wallace, *Pennsylvania.*

FELLOWS

Fellow in Classical Literature

Samuel Grant Oliphant,[1]   *New Jersey*

J S K Fellow in Mathematics

Clarence McCheyne Gordon,   *Pennsylvania*

Chancellor Green Fellow in Mental Science

George Herbert Stephens,   *Pennsylvania*

Class of 1860 Fellow in Experimental Science

Elwood Waite Elder,   *Ohio*

Boudinot Fellow in Modern Languages

John Preston Hoskins,   *Pennsylvania*

Boudinot Fellow in History

Alfred Pearce Dennis,   *Maryland*

E M Fellow in Biological Science

William Post Herrick,   *New York*

Class of 1877 University Fellow in Biology

Albert Chauncey Eycleshymer[2]   *Michigan*

South East Club University Fellow in Social Science

Winthrop More Daniels,[3] '88,   *Ohio*

Fellow in Social Science

John Haughton Coney, '85,   *Ohio*

---

[1] Resigned.   [2] University of Michigan

[3] Resigned

University Fellow in Archæology

Edward Waterman Evans, Jr.,   *New Jersey*

Fellows in Oratory

George Riddle Wallace,   *Pennsylvania*
George Post Wheeler,   *Pennsylvania*

Special Fellow in Biology

Francis Ernest Lloyd,[1]   *Pennsylvania*

PRIZEMEN

Class of 1859 Prize in English Literature

Edward Waterman Evans, Jr.,   *New Jersey*

George Potts Bible Prizes

William Littell Everitt,   *New Jersey*
Phineas Barbour Kennedy,   *New Jersey*

Alexander Guthrie McCosh Prize

Edward Waterman Evans, Jr.,   *New Jersey*

Atwater Prize in Political Science

James Henry Dunham,   *New Jersey*

Theodore Cuyler Prize in Economics

Thomas Ferguson McNair,   *Pennsylvania*

Class of 1869 Prize in Ethics[2]

George Herbert Stephens,   *Pennsylvania*

Joline Prize in American Political History

James Cowden Meyers,   *Pennsylvania*

Class of 1876 Prize for Debate in Political Science

Samuel Semple,   *Pennsylvania*

[1] Resigned
[2] With honorable mention of Ambrose White Vernon of New Jersey.

Lynde Prize Debate

Clisosophic Society

Alfred Pearce Dennis,	*Maryland*
James Henry Dunham,	*New Jersey*
Samuel Semple,	*Pennsylvania*

American Whig Society

James Cowden Meyers,	*Pennsylvania*
George Riddle Wallace,	*Pennsylvania*
Samuel Wasson,	*Pennsylvania*

Lynde Debate Prizemen

Samuel Semple,	First Prize
James Cowden Meyers,	Second Prize
George Riddle Wallace,	Third Prize

Baird Prizemen

Wilson Aull, *Missouri*,	Baird Prize
Hugh McNinch, *Pennsylvania*,	Oratory
Phineas Barbour Kennedy, *New Jersey*,	Delivery
Edward Waterman Evans, Jr , *New Jersey*,	Poetry
Ambrose White Vernon, *New Jersey*, *First*,	Disputation
James Cowden Meyers, *Pennsylvania*, *Second*,	

Junior Honors

Irving Whitall Street, *Ohio*,	First Honor

Junior Orators

Clisosophic Society

Courtlandt Patterson Butler,	*New Jersey*
Edward Dickinson Duffield,	*New Jersey*
William Kelly Prentice,	*New York*
John Glover Wilson,	*Maryland*

American Whig Society

Joseph Miller Huston,	*Pennsylvania*
Bowdre Phinizy,	*Georgia*
Charles Irvin Truby,	*Pennsylvania*
Clinton Tyler Wood,	*North Dakota*

Junior Orator Medalists

Bowdre Phinizy,	First Medal
Joseph Miller Huston,	Second Medal
Edward Dickinson Duffield,	Third Medal
William Kelly Prentice,	Fourth Medal

PRIZEMEN

Maclean Prize

Clinton Tyler Wood,	*North Dakota*

Dickinson Prize

James Peter King,	*Ontario*

Thomas B Wanamaker English Prize

Irving Whitall Street,	*Ohio*

Class of 1870 English Prizes

Elmer Baldwin Cole, *New Jersey,*	Anglo-Saxon
Irving Whitall Street, *Ohio,*	English Literature

Frederick Barnard White Prize in Architecture

Benjamin Vroom White,	*New Jersey*

Sophomore Honors

Class of 1861 Prize

James Warren Ritchey,	*Indiana*

Francis Biddle Prize

Charles Bertram Newton,	*Pennsylvania*

Class of 1870 English Prize

Jesse Benedict Carter,	*New York*

Stinnecke Scholar

Jesse Benedict Carter,   *New York*

Freshman Honors

Albert Thomas Davis, *New Jersey*,   First Honor

ENTRANCE EXAMINATION PRIZES

Alumni Prize in New York City

Albert Thomas Davis,   *New Jersey*

George W Childs Prize in Philadelphia

Frank Strickler Henderson,   *Pennsylvania*

In Albany

Boyd Van Benthuysen,   *New York*

In Chicago

John Crosby Neely,   *Illinois*

In Wilkes-Barre

Horace Day,   *Pennsylvania*

In Pittsburg

George Dickson Edwards,   *Pennsylvania*

1892

Senior Honors

FIRST GROUP   *Magna cum laude*

Albert Frost Earnshaw,	*New York*
Le Roy Gresham,	*Maryland*
James Peter King, *Ontario*,	English Salutatory
Bowdre Phinizy,	*Georgia*
William Kelly Prentice, *New York*,	Valedictory Oration
Irving Whitall Street,	*Ohio*
John Glover Wilson, *Maryland*,	Latin Salutatory
Clinton Tyler Wood,	*North Dakota*

Special Honors

CLASSICS — Elmer Baldwin Cole, *New Jersey,* Henry Clay Havens, *New Jersey;* William Kelly Prentice, *New York,* Clinton Tyler Wood, *North Dakota.*

MATHEMATICS AND MATHFMAIICAL SCIENCE — Herman Stearns Davis, *Delaware,* Walter Livingston Wright, Jr , *New Jersey*

MODERN LANGUAGES—Williamson Updike Vreeland, *New Jersey*

ARCHÆOLOGY AND ART — Benjamin Vroom White, *New Jersey.*

MFNTAL PHILOSOPHY — Caspar Wistar Hodge, Jr., *New Jersey,* James Peter King, *Ontario,* Irving Whitall Street, *Ohio,* Clinton Tyler Wood, *North Dakota.*

HISTORY AND POLITICAL SCIFNCF—Bowdre Phinizy, *Georgia,* John Glover Wilson, *Maryland,* Percy Wilson, *Montana*

NATURAL SCIENCE—Marcus Stults Farr, *New Jersey*

FELLOWS[1]

Fellows in Classical Literature

Henry Clay Havens,	*New Jersey*
William Kelly Prentice,	*New York*

Chancellor Green Fellow in Mental Science

James Peter King,	*Ontario*

Class of 1860 Fellow in Experimental Science

Walter Livingston Wright, Jr.,	*New Jersey*

Boudinot Fellow in Modern Languages

Williamson Updike Vreeland,	*New Jersey*

Boudinot Fellow in History

Max Farrand.	*New Jersey*

E M. Fellow in Biological Science

John Young Graham,	*Wisconsin*

[1] The J. S K. Mathematical Fellowship not awarded

Class of 1877 University Fellow in Biology

Marcus Stults Fair, *New Jersey*

South East Club University Fellow in Social Science

Alfred Pearce Dennis, '91, *Maryland*

University Fellow in Archæology

Howard Crosby Butler, *New York*

Fellows in Oratory

George Post Wheeler, '91, *Pennsylvania*
Harry Franklin Covington, *Maryland*

PRIZEMEN

Class of 1859 Prize in English Literature

Irving Whitall Street, *Ohio*

George Potts Bible Prizes

Cassius Edwin Bixler, *Pennsylvania*
James Peter King, *Ontario*

Alexander Guthrie McCosh Prize

James Peter King, *Ontario*

Atwater Prize in Political Science

Charles Ogden Mudge, *New Jersey*

Theodore Cuyler Prize in Economics

John Glover Wilson, *Maryland*

Class of 1869 Prize in Ethics[1]

Caspar Wistar Hodge, Jr, *New Jersey*

Joline Prize in American Political History

Charles Irvin Truby, *Pennsylvania*

Class of 1876 Prize for Debate in Political Science

Le Roy Gresham, *Maryland*

---

[1] With honorable mention of Albert Frost Farnshaw of New York

Frederick Barnard White Prize in Architecture

Edgar Trotter Van Deusen,   *New York*

Special Bible Prize

William Harris, Jr ,   *New Jersey*

Special Prize in Shakespeare

Harry Franklin Covington,   *Maryland*

Lynde Prize Debate

Cliosophic Society

Howland Hanson,   *New Jersey*
William Kelly Prentice,   *New York*
Irving Whitall Street,   *Ohio*

American Whig Society

John Menifee Brennan,   *Kentucky*
Bowdre Phinizy,   *Georgia*
Clinton Tyler Wood,   *North Dakota*

Lynde Debate Prizemen

Bowdre Phinizy,   First Prize
William Kelly Prentice,   Second Prize
Howland Hanson,   Third Prize

Baird Prizemen

Le Roy Gresham, *Maryland*,   Baird Prize
William Kelly Prentice, *New York*,   Oratory
Bowdre Phinizy, *Georgia*,   Delivery
Ralph Dutfield Small, *Massachusetts*,   Poetry
Harry Franklin Covington, *Maryland, First*,
Edward Dickinson Duffield, *New Jersey, Second*,   Disputation

Junior Honors

Jesse Benedict Carter, *New York*,   First Honor

Junior Orators

Cliosophic Society

Jesse Benedict Carter,	*New York*
Benjamin Brandreth McAlpin,	*New York*
Charles Bertram Newton,	*Pennsylvania*
Bertram Van Dyck Post,	*Syria*

American Whig Society

Abram Piatt Andrew, Jr ,	*Indiana*
Horace Lyman Brown Henderson,	*Pennsylvania*
John Washington Nicely,	*Indiana*
Alexander Marshall Thompson,	*Minnesota*

Junior Orator Medalists

Alexander Marshall Thompson,	First Medal
Benjamin Brandreth McAlpin,	Second Medal
John Washington Nicely,	Third Medal
Bertram Van Dyck Post,	Fourth Medal

Prizemen

Maclean Prize

Charles Bertram Newton,	*Pennsylvania*

Dickinson Prize

Guy Allan Tawney,	*Minnesota*

Thomas B. Wanamaker English Prize

Jesse Benedict Carter,	*New York*

Class of 1870 English Prizes

Jesse Benedict Carter,	*New York*,	Anglo-Saxon [1]
William Ashenhurst Dunn,	*Ohio*,	English Literature

Stinnecke Scholar

Jesse Benedict Carter,	*New York*

---

[1] With honorable mention of William Ashenhurst Dunn of Ohio

Sophomore Honors
Class of 1861 Prize
Edward Rutledge Robbins, *New Jersey*

Francis Biddle Prize
Benjamin William M'Cready Sykes, *New Jersey*

Class of 1870 English Prize
Albert Thomas Davis, *New Jersey*

Freshman Honors
Arthur Register Wells, *Iowa*, First Honor

Entrance Examination Prizes
Alumni Prize in New York City
Walter Gillette Libby, *New Jersey*

George W Childs Prize in Philadelphia
Wilbur Marshall Urban, *Pennsylvania*

In Albany
Henry Augustus McNulty, *New Jersey*

In Chicago
Samuel Howe, *Illinois*

In Wilkes-Barre and Scranton
Lucius Carter Kennedy, *Pennsylvania*

In Pittsburg
Warren Ilsley Seymour, *Pennsylvania*

In Harrisburg
William John Bone, *Pennsylvania*

1893
Senior Honors

First Group *Magna cum laude*

Jesse Benedict Carter, *New York*,	Latin Salutatory
Samuel Cochran,	*New Jersey*
William Ashenhurst Dunn, *Ohio*,	English Salutatory
Cortlandt Van Rensselaer Hodge,	*New Jersey*
Herbert Ludlum Winans,	*New York*

Bertram Van Dyck Post,[1] *Syria*,	Valedictory Oration
Abram Piatt Andrew, Jr , *Indiana*,[2]	Valedictory Oration

Special Honors

CLASSICS—Jesse Benedict Carter, *New York*

MATHEMATICS AND MATHEMATICAL SCIENCE—John Nevius Dodd, *New York,* Frederick Stanton Elder, *Kansas,* James Warren Ritchey, *Indiana,* John Featherer Wilkinson, *New Jersey.*

MENTAL PHILOSOPHY—Abram Piatt Andrew, Jr , *Indiana,* Lee Montgomery, *Missouri,* Guy Allan Tawney, *Minnesota.*

HISTORY AND POLITICAL SCIENCE—John Lee Tildsley, *New York*

NATURAL SCIENCE—Joseph Hervey Buchanan, *New Jersey,* Herbert Ludlum Winans, *New York*

ENGLISH—William Ashenhurst Dunn, *Ohio,* Charles Bertram Newton, *Pennsylvania*

FELLOWS

Fellow in Classical Literature

Jesse Benedict Carter,	*New York*

---

[1] Post and Andrew of the Second Group, *cum laude.* Mr Post was excused from delivering the Valedictory on account of ill health *Minutes of the Faculty,* May 3, 1893

[2] Alternate

J S K Fellow in Mathematics

John Nevius Dodd,   *New York*

Chancellor Green Fellow in Mental Science

Guy Allan Tawney,   *Minnesota*

Class of 1860 Fellow in Experimental Science

James Warren Ritchey,   *Indiana*

Boudinot Fellow in Modern Languages

Joseph Albright Henry,   *New Jersey*

Boudinot Fellow in History

John Lee Tildsley,   *New York*

Class of 1877 University Fellow in Biology

Alvin Davison,[1]   *Tennessee*

South East Club University Fellow in Social Science

Max Farrand, '92,   *New Jersey*

University Fellow in Archæology

Nicholas Evertson Crosby,   *New York*

University Fellow in English

Thomas Marc Parrott, '88.   *Ohio*

Special Fellow in English

William Ashenhurst Dunn,   *Ohio*

PRIZEMEN

Class of 1859 Prize in English Literature[2]

William Ashenhurst Dunn,   *Ohio*

George Potts Bible Prizes

Charles Trowbridge Riggs,   *Turkey*
Charles William Ottley,   *Georgia*

[1] B S , National College, Ohio

[2] With honorable mention of Robert Thomas Sloss of New Jersey

Alexander Guthrie McCosh Prize

Guy Allan Tawney   *Minnesota*

Atwater Prize in Political Science

John Lee Tildsley,   *New York*

Theodore Cuyler Prize in Economics

John Lee Tildsley,   *New York*

Class of 1869 Prize in Ethics [1]

Lee Montgomery,   *Missouri*

Joline Prize in American Political History

Marshall Harrington,   *Ohio*

Class of 1876 Prize for Debate in Political Science

Jesse Benedict Carter,   *New York*

Lynde Prize Debate

Cliosophic Society

Isaac Wingerd Byers,   *Pennsylvania*
Guy Allan Tawney,   *Minnesota*
John Lee Tildsley,   *New York*

American Whig Society

Thomas Spencer Crago,   *Pennsylvania*
Jay Falconer Ewing,   *Iowa*
John Washington Nicely,   *Indiana*

Lynde Debate Prizemen

John Washington Nicely,   First Prize
Thomas Spencer Crago,   Second Prize
Jay Falconer Ewing,   Third Prize

Baird Prizemen

Bertram Van Dyck Post, *Syria*,   Baird Prize
Guy Allan Tawney, *Minnesota*,   Oratory

---

[1] With honorable mention of John Featherer Wilkinson of New Jersey

James Beveridge, *New York,*   Delivery
William Ashenhurst Dunn, *Ohio,*   Poetry
Jay Falconer Ewing, *Iowa, First,*
Charles William Ottley, *Georgia, Second,*   Disputation

Junior Honors[1]

JUNIOR ORATORS

Cliosophic Society

George Stewart McCague,   *Nebraska*
Donald MacColl,   *New York*
Alexander McGaffin,   *Ireland*
Benjamin William M'Cready Sykes,   *New Jersey*

American Whig Society

James Maclin Brodnax,   *Tennessee*
Herbert Herschel Fisher,   *Illinois*
Ernest Farwell Keigwin,   *Delaware*
Edward Reed Laughlin,   *Pennsylvania*

Junior Orator Medalists

Alexander McGaffin,   First Medal
Donald MacColl,   Second Medal
Ernest Farwell Keigwin,   Third Medal
Herbert Herschel Fisher,   Fourth Medal

PRIZEMEN

Maclean Prize

Benjamin William M'Cready Sykes,   *New Jersey*

Dickinson Prize

Joseph William Lester Jones,   *New Jersey*

Thomas B. Wanamaker English Prize

Albert Thomas Davis,   *New Jersey*

---

[1] No award of First Honor Prize.

Class of 1870 English Prizes

George Stewart McCague, *Nebraska*,   Anglo-Saxon
Samuel Wardwell Kinney, *New York*, English Literature

Frederick Barnard White Prize in Architecture

Benjamin William M'Cready Sykes,   *New Jersey*

Special Prize in Histology

Ulric Dahlgren,   *New Jersey*

Sophomore Honors

Class of 1861 Prize

William Douglas Ward,   *New York*

Francis Biddle Prize

Wilbur Marshall Urban,   *Pennsylvania*

Class of 1870 English Prize

Andrew Clerk Imbrie,   *New York*

Freshman Honors

Frederick William Loetscher, *Iowa*,   First Honor

Entrance Examination Prizes

Alumni Prize in New York City

Charles Byron Bostwick,   *New York*
Louis Herbert Gray,   *New Jersey*

George W Childs Prizes in Philadelphia

Ralph Barton Perry, *Pennsylvania*,   Academic
Frederick Curwen Leas, *Pennsylvania*, School of Science

In Wilkes-Barre and Scranton

Thomas Henry Atherton Stites,   *Pennsylvania*

In Pittsburg

Samuel Wilson Miller, Jr,   *Pennsylvania*

In Harrisburg

William Henry Muser,   *Pennsylvania*

In Washington, D C

Wallace Donald McLean,   *District of Columbia*

1894

Senior Honors

FIRST GROUP *Magna cum laude*

Charles Merritt Cartwright,   *Ohio*
James Carpenter Coleman, Jr.,   *New York*
Albert Thomas Davis,   *New Jersey*
George Dickson Edwards,   *Pennsylvania*
Paul Erdman, *New Jersey*,   English Salutatory
Charles Sumner Havens,   *New Jersey*
Charles Alexander Robinson, *New York*, Latin Salutatory
George Handy Wailes,   *Maryland*

Alexander McGaffin, *Ireland*, Valedictory Oration

Special Honors

PHILOSOPHY. *High Honors*—Joseph William Lester Jones, *New Jersey,* William Hoge McCartney, *Pennsylvania,* Edward Johnson Russell, *New Jersey,* Benjamin William M'Cready Sykes, *Pennsylvania*

HISTORY, JURISPRUDENCE AND POLITICS. *High Honors*—Charles Merritt Cartwright, *Ohio,* George Dickson Edwards, *Pennsylvania;* Henry King Siebeneck, *Pennsylvania.* *Honors*—Charles Howard McIlwain, *Pennsylvania.*

CLASSICS. *High Honors*—Charles Sumner Havens, *New Jersey,* Charles Alexander Robinson, *New York,* Henry Mandlebert Sheldon, *New York,* William Ring Woodruff, *New Jersey* *Honors*—Arthur Holland Wadsworth, *New York*

MODERN LANGUAGES *High Honors*—Murray Peabody Brush, *Ohio;* George Madison Priest, *Kentucky.*

ENGLISH *High Honors*—Samuel Wardwell Kinney, *New York* *Honors*—Karl George, *New York*

MATHEMATICS. *High Honors*—Edward Rutledge Robbins, *New Jersey*

PHYSICAL SCIENCE. *Honors*—Alden Matthews Califf, *Pennsylvania*

NATURAL SCIENCE *Honors*—Ulric Dahlgren, *New Jersey*, Daniel Pratt, *New York*, Ernest Coniston Waterhouse, *Hawaiian Islands.*

FELLOWS

Fellow in Classical Literature

Charles Alexander Robinson, *New York*

J S K Fellow in Mathematics

Edward Rutledge Robbins, *New Jersey*

Chancellor Green Fellow in Mental Science

Joseph William Lester Jones, *New Jersey*

Class of 1860 Fellow in Experimental Science

Frank Forrester Thompson, *Pennsylvania*

Boudinot Fellow in Modern Languages

George Madison Priest, *Kentucky*

Boudinot Fellow in History

Charles Merritt Cartwright,[1] *Ohio*

E M. Fellow in Biological Science

Ulric Dahlgren, *New Jersey*

Class of 1877 University Fellow in Biology

Frederick Clark Paulmier, *New Jersey*

PRIZEMEN

Class of 1859 Prize in English Literature

Benjamin William M'Cready Sykes, *New Jersey*

---

[1] Resigned

George Potts Bible Prizes

Robert Bonner Jack,   *Pennsylvania*
Ernest Farwell Keigwin,   *Delaware*

Alexander Guthrie McCosh Prize

Benjamin William M'Cready Sykes,   *New Jersey*

Atwater Prize in Political Science

John Albert Murray,   *New York*

Theodore Cuyler Prize in Economics

Charles Merritt Cartwright,   *Ohio*

Class of 1869 Prize in Ethics

Horace Day,   *Pennsylvania*

Jolme Prize in American Political History

Cummings Waldo Cherry,   *Pennsylvania*

Class of 1876 Prize for Debate in Political Science

Donald MacColl,   *New York*

New York Herald Prize

Sidney Radwell Yarrow,   *Massachusetts*

Frederick Barnard White Prize in Architecture

Benjamin William M'Cready Sykes,   *New Jersey*

LYNDE PRIZE DEBATE
Chosophic Society

Donald MacColl,   *New York*
Benjamin William M'Cready Sykes,   *New Jersey*
Charles Roger Watson,   *Egypt*

American Whig Society

James Shaw Campbell,   *Pennsylvania*
Grant Colfax Fox,   *New York*
Ernest Farwell Keigwin,   *Delaware*

Benjamin William M'Cready Sykes,	First Prize
Donald MacColl,	Second Prize
Charles Roger Watson,	Third Prize

BAIRD PRIZEMEN

Alexander McGaffin, *Ireland*,	Baird Prize
Benjamin William M'Cready Sykes, *New Jersey*,	Oratory
Edward Reed Laughlin, *Pennsylvania*,	Delivery
Benjamin William M'Cready Sykes, *New Jersey*,	Poetry
Donald MacColl, *New York*, *First*,	Disputation
Charles Roger Watson, *Egypt*, *Second*,	

Junior Honors

John Thomson Faris, *Pennsylvania*,	First Honor

JUNIOR ORATORS

Cliosophic Society

Willis Howard Butler,	*New York*
Ray Harrison Carter,	*Pennsylvania*
John Collings Caton,	*England*
Benjamin Lewis Hirshfield,	*Ohio*

American Whig Society

Andrew Clerk Imbrie,	*New York*
Edwin Mark Norris,	*Iowa*
Wilbur Marshall Urban,	*Pennsylvania*
Howard Erskine White,	*New York*

Junior Orator Medalists

Howard Erskine White,	First Medal
Ray Harrison Carter,	Second Medal
Andrew Clerk Imbrie,	Third Medal
Willis Howard Butler,	Fourth Medal

Prizemen
Maclean Prize
Benjamin Lewis Hirshfield,　　　　　　　　*Ohio*

Dickinson Prize[1]
John Forsyth Crawford,　　　　　　　　*Syria*

Thomas B Wanamaker English Prize
Henry Augustus McNulty,　　　　　　　　*New Jersey*

Class of 1870 English Prizes
Henry Buck Master, *Pennsylvania*,　　　　Anglo-Saxon
John Thomson Faris, *Pennsylvania*,　　　English Literature

Special Prize in Histology
Raymond Lynde Wadhams,　　　　　　　　*Pennsylvania*

Sophomore Honors
Class of 1861 Prize
Albert Howe Lybyer,　　　　　　　　*Indiana*

Francis Biddle Prize
Edward Strong Worcester,　　　　　　　　*Vermont*

Class of 1870 English Prize[2]
Frederick William Loetscher,　　　　　　*Iowa*

Stinnecke Scholar
Charles Byron Bostwick,　　　　　　　　*New York*

Freshman Honors
Frederick Nevins Jessup, *Syria*,　　　　First Honor

Entrance Examination Prizes
Alumni Prize in New York City
Percy Robert Colwell,　　　　　　　　*New York*

---

[1] With honorable mention of Wilbur Marshall Urban of Pennsylvania
[2] With honorable mention of John Moore Trout of Delaware

George W Childs Prizes in Philadelphia

Wayne MacVeagh Wilson, *Pennsylvania,*   Academic
Thomas Hall Ingham, *Pennsylvania,*   School of Science

In Northeast Pennsylvania

Nicholas Stahl,   *Pennsylvania*

In Pittsburg

Daniel Edward Nevin,   *Pennsylvania*

1895

Senior Honors

FIRST GROUP   *Magna cum laude*

John Forsyth Crawford,   *Syria*
Alfred Hayes, Jr ,   *Pennsylvania*
Daniel Fellows Platt, *New Jersey,*   English Salutatory
Joseph Curtis Sloane,   *Pennsylvania*
Wilbur Marshall Urban,   *Pennsylvania*
William Douglas Ward, *New York,*   Latin Salutatory
Arthur Register Wells,   *Iowa*

Richard Daniel Hatch,[1] *New York,*   Valedictory Oration

Special Honors

PHILOSOPHY.   *High Honors* — John Forsyth Crawford, *Syria,* Daniel Weaver Dexter, *New York,* Edwin Mark Norris, *Iowa,* Wilbur Marshall Urban, *Pennsylvania*

HISTORY, JURISPRUDENCE AND POLITICS   *High Honors*— Alfred Hayes, Jr., *Pennsylvania   Honors* — Daniel Fellows Platt, *New Jersey.*

CLASSICS   *High Honors* — Joseph Curtis Sloane, *Pennsylvania,* Louis Clayton Woodruff, *Connecticut. Honors* — Robert Patterson Harris, *New Jersey*

ENGLISH.   *High Honors* — Henry Buck Master, *Pennsylvania*

---

[1] Of the Second Group, *cum laude*

Natural Science   *High Honors*—Curtis Smiley Foster, *Pennsylvania.*

Mathematics   *High Honors* — William Douglas Ward, *New York*

School of Science

Bachelor of Science Course   *High Honors*

Orrel Ardrey Parker,	*Ohio*

Honors

Ralph Waldo Bailey,	*New Jersey*
Henry Matthews Canby,	*Delaware*
Edwin Snow La Fetra,	*District of Columbia*

Civil Engineering Course   *Honors*

George Fisher Barton,	*New Jersey*
Carleton Curtis,	*New York*
Charles Kellerman,	*Pennsylvania*
Charles Arthur Poole,	*New York*

Fellows[1]

Fellow in Classical Literature

Louis Clayton Woodruff,	*Connecticut*

J. S K Fellow in Mathematics

William Douglas Ward,	*New York*

Chancellor Green Fellow in Mental Science

Wilbur Marshall Urban,	*Pennsylvania*

Class of 1860 Fellow in Experimental Science

Howard Doty Carpenter,	*Massachusetts*

Boudinot Fellow in History

Dexter Mason Ferry Weeks,	*New York*

Class of 1877 University Fellow in Biology

George Irving Adams,[2]	*Kansas*

[1] No award of the Boudinot Modern Language Fellowship, or of the E M Biological Fellowship

[2] Kansas University

South East Club University Fellow in Social Science
Ernest Ludlow Bogart, '90,   *New York*

PRIZEMEN

Class of 1859 Prize in English Literature
Henry Buck Master,   *Pennsylvania*

George Potts Bible Prizes
Charles Beach Condit,   *New Jersey*
Edgar Mason Smead,   *New York*

Alexander Guthrie McCosh Prize
John Forsyth Crawford,   *Syria*

Atwater Prize in Political Science
Harry Morgan Post,   *New York*

Theodore Cuyler Prize in Economics
Robert Edwin Ross,   *Illinois*

Class of 1869 Prize in Ethics
Daniel Weaver Dexter,   *New York*

Joline Prize in American Political History
Edward Henry Hoos,   *New Jersey*

New York Herald Prize
Arthur Dunn,   *Illinois*

Frederick Barnard White Prize in Architecture
Henry Buck Master,   *Pennsylvania*

LYNDE PRIZE DEBATE

Cliosophic Society

Selden Long Haynes,   *Indian Territory*
Benjamin Lewis Hirshfield,   *Ohio*
Frederick Wheeler Lewis,   *Kansas*

American Whig Society

William Foster Burns,	*Illinois*
Alfred Hayes, Jr ,	*Pennsylvania*
Joseph William Park,	*Mississippi*

Lynde Debate Prizemen

Benjamin Lewis Hirshfield,	First Prize
Frederick Wheeler Lewis,	Second Prize
William Foster Burns,	Third Prize

Baird Prizemen

Andrew Clerk Imbrie, *New York*,	Baird Prize
Victor Herbert Lukens, *New Jersey*,	Oratory
Willis Howard Butler, *New York*,	Delivery
Wilbur Marshall Urban, *Pennsylvania*,	Poetry
Joseph William Park, *Mississippi*, *First*,	Disputation
Alfred Hayes, Jr , *Pennsylvania*, *Second*,	

Junior Honors

Frederick William Loetscher, *Iowa*,	First Honor

Junior Orators
Cliosophic Society

John James Moment,	*Ontario*
John Moore Trout,	*Delaware*
George Henry Waters,	*New York*
Charles Wesley Wisner, Jr.,	*Maryland*

American Whig Society

Edward William Hamilton,	*New York*
Frederick William Loetscher,	*Iowa*
Edward Bates Turner,	*Iowa*
Edward Strong Worcester,	*Vermont*

Junior Orator Medalists

John James Moment,	First Medal
George Henry Waters,	Second Medal
John Moore Trout,	Third Medal
Edward William Hamilton,	Fourth Medal

PRIZEMEN

Maclean Prize
Edward Strong Worcester,   *Vermont*

Dickinson Prize
John Moore Trout,   *Delaware*

Thomas B. Wanamaker English Prize
Frederick William Loetscher,   *Iowa*

Class of 1870 English Prizes
Frederick William Loetscher, *Iowa*,	Anglo-Saxon
John Moore Trout, *Delaware*,	English Literature

Special Prize in Histology
William Noble Keller,   *Iowa*

Stinnecke Scholar
Charles Byron Bostwick,   *New York*

Sophomore Honors

Class of 1861 Prize
Henry Norris Russell,   *New York*

Francis Biddle Prize
Arthur Willis Leonard,   *Ohio*

Class of 1876 Prize for Debate in Political Science
Robert Fulton Sterling,   *Pennsylvania*

Class of 1870 English Prize
John Henry Keener,   *Pennsylvania*

Freshman Honors

Howard Herr Yocum, *Pennsylvania,* First Honor

ENTRANCE EXAMINATION PRIZES

Alumni Prize in New York City

Ezra Parmelee Prentice, *New York*

George W Childs Prizes in Philadelphia

Edgar Marvin Clark, *Pennsylvania,* Academic
Henry Hutton Kennedy, Jr , *Pennsylvania,* School of Science

In Chicago

Carl Seward Reed, *Illinois*

In Newark

Albert Windemuth Harris, *New Jersey,* Academic
Robert Stewart Brooks, *New Jersey,* School of Science

1896

Senior Honors

FIRST GROUP *Magna cum laude*

Philip Hudson Churchman, *New Jersey*
Frank Lindley Critchlow, *England*
Louis Herbert Gray, *New Jersey*
Edward Blanchard Hodge, Jr , *New Jersey*
Frederick William Loetscher, *Iowa,* Latin Salutatory
Albert Howe Lybyer, *Indiana,* English Salutatory
Charles Bell McMullen, *Missouri*
William Arnot Mather, *New York*
John James Moment, *Ontario*
Ralph Barton Perry, *New York*
John Moore Trout, *Delaware*
Edward Strong Worcester, *Vermont,* Valedictory Oration

Special Honors

PHILOSOPHY. *High Honors*—William Edmund Lampe, *Maryland,* Albert Howe Lybyer, *Indiana,* John James Moment,

Ontario, John Moore Trout, *Delaware,* Robert McNutt Mc-Elroy, *Missouri.* *Honors*—William Furman Doty, *District of Columbia,* Alexander Nelson Easton, *New Jersey.*

HISTORY, JURISPRUDENCE AND POLITICS. *High Honors*—Frederick William Loetscher, *Iowa,* Albert Howe Lybyer, *Indiana,* Robert McNutt McElroy, *Missouri.* *Honors*—Henry Beard Armes, *District of Columbia*

CLASSICS *High Honors*—Louis Herbert Gray, *New Jersey.*

MODERN LANGUAGES. *High Honors* — Edward Hodge Bishop, *New Jersey,* Philip Hudson Churchman, *New Jersey,* Theodore Clifford Coe, *New Jersey.* *Honors*—Jacob Newton Beam, *Pennsylvania;* William Henry Musser, *Pennsylvania*

ENGLISH. *High Honors*—Herbert Ure, *New Jersey*

MATHEMATICS AND PHYSICS. *High Honors* — Robert Lincoln Litch, *Pennsylvania,* Stanley Chester Reese, *Pennsylvania.*

SCHOOL OF SCIENCE

Bachelor of Science Course *Honors*

William Bush,	*Delaware*

Civil Engineering Course *Honors*

Albert Irving Payne,	*New York*
Lloyd Llewellyn Smith,	*New Jersey*
Francis Gray Stewart,	*New York*

FELLOWS[1]

Fellow in Classical Literature

Louis Herbert Gray,	*New Jersey*

J. S K Fellow in Mathematics

Stanley Chester Reese,	*Pennsylvania*

Chancellor Green Fellow in Mental Science

John Moore Trout,	*Delaware*

Class of 1860 Fellow in Experimental Science

Robert Lincoln Litch,	*Pennsylvania*

[1] No award of E M Fellowship in Biology

Boudinot Fellow in Modern Languages
Edward Hodge Bishop,   *New Jersey*

Boudinot Fellow in History
Robert McNutt McElroy,   *Missouri*

Class of 1877 University Fellow in Biology
Alfred Abel Doolittle,   *China*

South East Club University Fellow in Social Science
Joseph William Park, '95,   *Mississippi*

Prizemen

Class of 1859 Prize in English Literature
Samuel Robert Spriggs,   *New York*

George Potts Bible Prizes
Leroy Kirkman,   *New York*
Samuel Robert Spriggs,   *New York*

Alexander Guthrie McCosh Prize
William Arnot Mather,   *New York*

Atwater Prize in Political Science
Edward William Hamilton,   *New York*

Theodore Cuyler Prize in Economics
Albert Howe Lybyer,   *Indiana*

Class of 1869 Prize in Ethics
John Moore Trout.   *Delaware*

Joline Prize in American Political History
Alfred Lewis Pinneo Dennis,   *New York*

New York Herald Prize
Henry Beard Armes,   *District of Columbia*

Frederick Barnard White Prize in Architecture
William Woodburn Potter,   *Pennsylvania*

Lynde Prize Debate

Cliosophic Society

William Furman Doty,	*District of Columbia*
Alexander Nelson Easton,	*New Jersey*
Albert Howe Lybyer,	· *Indiana*

American Whig Society

Edward William Hamilton,	*New York*
Frederick William Loetscher,	*Iowa*
Robert McNutt McElroy,	*Missouri*

Lynde Debate Prizemen

Robert McNutt McElroy,	First Prize
Frederick William Loetscher,	Second Prize
Edward William Hamilton,	Third Prize

Baird Prizemen

John Moore Trout, *Delaware,*	Baird Prize
John James Moment, *Ontario,*	Oratory
Ralph Barton Perry, *New York,*	Delivery
Francis Charles MacDonald, *Pennsylvania,*	Poetry
Robert McNutt McElroy, *Missouri, First,*	Disputation
Alexander Nelson Easton, *New Jersey, Second,*	

Junior Honors

Henry Norris Russell, *New York,*	First Honor

Junior Orators

Cliosophic Society

Frank Bertine Cowan,	*New York*
Wilfred McIlvaine Post,	*Syria*
Henry Ford Stockwell,	*New Jersey*
Edward Cameron Thompson,	*New York*

American Whig Society

John Henry Keener,	*Pennsylvania*
Arthur Willis Leonard,	*Ohio*
Frank Montgomery Wood, Jr ,	*North Dakota*
Charles Gorman Richards,	*Pennsylvania*

Junior Orator Medalists

Wilfred McIlvaine Post,	First Medal
Charles Gorman Richards,	Second Medal
John Henry Keener,	Third Medal
Frank Bertine Cowan,	Fourth Medal

PRIZEMEN

Maclean Prize

Arthur Willis Leonard,	*Ohio*

Dickinson Prize[1]

Robert Comin,	*Ohio*

Thomas B Wanamaker English Prize

John Henry Keener,	*Pennsylvania*

Class of 1870 English Prizes

Arthur Willis Leonard, *Ohio*,	Anglo-Saxon
John Henry Keener, *Pennsylvania*,	English Literature

Sophomore Honors

Class of 1861 Prize

Howard Herr Yocum,	*Pennsylvania*

Francis Biddle Prize

Meade Tyrrell Williams,	*Missouri*

Class of 1870 English Prize

Howard Herr Yocum,	*Pennsylvania*

[1] With honorable mention of John Henry Keener of Pennsylvania

Class of 1876 Prize for Debate in Political Science
Milton Floyd Loofbourrow,   *Ohio*

Freshman Honors

William Magill Schultz, *Pennsylvania*,   First Honor

Stinnecke Scholar
Richard Webster,   *New York*

Entrance Examination Prizes
Alumni Prize in New York City
Richard Webster,   *New York*

George W Childs Prize in Philadelphia[1]
Henry Blackiston Patton, *Pennsylvania*,   Academic

1897
Senior Honors[2]

First Group   *Insigni cum laude*
Henry Norris Russell, *New York*,   Latin Salutatory

Magna cum laude

Edward William Axson,	*New Jersey*
John Henry Nichols,	*New York*
Horace Greeley Padget,	*New York*
Austin McDowell Patterson,	*Ohio*
Nicholas Stahl,	*Pennsylvania*

John Henry Keener,[3] *Pennsylvania*,   Valedictory Oration

Special Honors

Philosophy   *High Honors*—John Henry Keener, *Penn-sylvania*.

---

[1] No award of School of Science Prize

[2] School of Science honormen not announced in the Faculty minutes

[3] Of the Second Group, *cum laude*

HISTORY, JURISPRUDENCE AND POLITICS—*High Honors*—George Howe, *South Carolina*.   *Honors*—Robert Comin, *Ohio*.

CLASSICS.   *High Honors*—Herschel Augustus Norris, *New Jersey*, Horace Greeley Padget, *New York;* Henry Van Cleaf, *New Jersey*

MODERN LANGUAGES   *High Honors*—Charles Francis Dunn, *Ohio*, John Henry Nichols, *New York*.

ENGLISH   *High Honors*—Arthur Willis Leonard, *Ohio*.

MATHEMATICS   *Highest Honors*—Henry Norris Russell, *New York*   *High Honors*—Nicholas Stahl, *Pennsylvania*.

PHYSICAL SCIENCE   *High Honors*—Edward William Axson, *New Jersey;* Henry Norris Russell, *New York;* Nicholas Stahl, *Pennsylvania*

SCHOOL OF SCIENCE

Civil Engineering Course

Sydney Wentworth Taylor, Jr, *Kansas*,   Honorary Oration

FELLOWS[1]

Fellow in Classical Literature

Horace Greeley Padget,   *New York*

J S K Fellow in Mathematics

Henry Norris Russell,   *New York*

Chancellor Green Fellow in Mental Science

John Henry Keener,   *Pennsylvania*

Class of 1860 Fellow in Experimental Science

Nicholas Stahl,   *Pennsylvania*

Boudinot Fellow in Modern Languages

John Henry Nichols,   *New York*

Boudinot Fellow in History

Frederick Walworth Brown,   *New Jersey*

---

[1] No award of the E. M Biological Fellowship

University Fellow in Archæology

Howard Crosby Butler, '92,   *New York*

Class of 1877 University Fellow in Biology

Elmer Samuel Riggs,[1]   *Kansas*

South East Club University Fellow in Social Science

Robert McNutt McElroy, '96,   *Missouri*

Special Fellow in Biology

Alfred Abel Doolittle, '96,   *China*

Thaw Fellow in Astronomy

Stanley Chester Reese, '96,   *Pennsylvania*

PRIZEMEN

Class of 1859 Prize in English Literature

Percy Robert Colwell,   *New York*

George Potts Bible Prizes

Thomas Sumption Minker,   *Pennsylvania*
Frederic Janvier Newton,   *India*

Alexander Guthrie McCosh Prize

Robert Lee Hallett,   *Delaware*

Atwater Prize in Political Science[2]

Henry Ford Stockwell,   *New Jersey*

Theodore Cuyler Prize in Economics

George Howe,   *South Carolina*

Class of 1869 Prize in Ethics

Robert Comin,   *Ohio*

Johne Prize in American Political History

Alfred Lewis Pinneo Dennis,[3]   *New York*

[1] B A , Kansas University.
[2] With honorable mention of George Harrington Kelly of Ohio
[3] Of the class of 1896

New York Herald Prize[1]

Robert Comin,   *Ohio*

Frederick Barnard White Prize in Architecture

John Barclay De Coursey,   *Pennsylvania*

National Society of the American Revolution Medal

Frank Montgomery Wood, Jr.,   *North Dakota*

LYNDE PRIZE DEBATE

Cliosophic Society

Samuel Stewart Yantis,   *Kentucky*
Henry Ford Stockwell,   *New Jersey*
William Boyd Ramsey,   *Ohio*

American Whig Society

Thomas St Clair Evans,   *Pennsylvania*
Robert Fulton Sterling,   *Pennsylvania*
Edward Graham Elliott,   *Tennessee*

Lynde Debate Prizemen

Robert Fulton Sterling,   First Prize
Henry Ford Stockwell,   Second Prize
Thomas St. Clair Evans,   Third Prize

BAIRD PRIZEMEN

Arthur Willis Leonard, *Ohio*,   Baird Prize
Wilfred McIlvaine Post, *Syria*,   Oratory
Edward Cameron Thompson, *New York*,   Delivery
Robert Fulton Sterling, *Pennsylvania, First*,
Henry Ford Stockwell, *New Jersey, Second*,   Disputation

Junior Honors

Frederic Leopold Johnson, *New Jersey*,
Howard Heir Yocum, *Pennsylvania*,   First Honor

---

[1] With honorable mention of Frederick Walworth Brown of New Jersey

Junior Orators

Cliosophic Society

George Alexander Armstrong,	*New York*
Robert Livingston Beecher,	*British Columbia*
Frederic Leopold Johnson,	*New Jersey*
Matthew Lowrie,	*Pennsylvania*

American Whig Society

Daniel Fickes Altland,	*Pennsylvania*
John Woolman Churchman,	*New Jersey*
Paul Curtis Martin,	*Ohio*
William Frank McCombs,	*Arkansas*

Junior Orator Medalists

Matthew Lowrie,	First Medal
Paul Curtis Martin,	Second Medal
Frederic Leopold Johnson,	Third Medal
George Alexander Armstrong,	Fourth Medal

Prizemen

Maclean Prize

Paul Curtis Martin,	*Ohio*

Dickinson Prize

William Emerson Nicely,	*Indiana*

Thomas B Wanamaker English Prize

Charles Harrison Hale,	*Mississippi*

Class of 1870 English Prizes

William Miller Gamble, *Pennsylvania*, Anglo-Saxon
Robert Livingston Beecher, *British Columbia*,

English Literature[1]

Class of 1876 Prize for Debate in Political Science

Howard Herr Yocum,	*Pennsylvania*

[1] With honorable mention of William Miller Gamble of Pennsylvania

Sophomore Honors
Class of 1861 Prize[1]
Warren Nelson Nevius,   *New Jersey*

Francis Biddle Prize[2]
Samuel Moore,   *New Jersey*

Class of 1870 English Prize
William Magill Schultz,   *Pennsylvania*

Stinnecke Scholar
Richard Webster,   *New York*

Freshman Honors
David Laurance Chambers, *District of Columbia,*   First Honor

ENTRANCE EXAMINATION PRIZES
Alumni Prize in New York City
William Van Buskirk,   *New York*

In Pittsburg
Samuel Bryan Scott,   *Pennsylvania*

In Harrisburg
Harry Steele Zimmerman,   *Pennsylvania*

In Missouri
Harry John Brandt,   *Missouri*

---

[1] With honorable mention of Oliver Dimon Kellogg of New Jersey.
[2] With honorable mention of George Wadsworth Gordon of Illinois.

1898

Senior Honors[1]

FIRST GROUP   *Magna cum laude*

Harry Elijah Belcher,	*New York*
Robert Smith Birch,	*Pennsylvania*
John Woolman Churchman,	*New Jersey*
Frederic Leopold Johnson,	*New Jersey*
Paul Curtis Martin, *Ohio*,	Valedictory Oration
Ezra Parmelee Prentice,	*New York*
Richard Frederic Lot Ridgway,	*New Jersey*
Philip Ely Robinson,	*Pennsylvania*
Howard Herr Yocum, *Pennsylvania*,	Latin Salutatory

Special Honors

PHILOSOPHY. *High Honors* — William Emerson Nicely, *Indiana*.

HISTORY, JURISPRUDENCE AND POLITICS   *High Honors*— Frederic Leopold Johnson, *New Jersey*, Paul Curtis Martin, *Ohio*, Howard Herr Yocum, *Pennsylvania*

CLASSICS. *High Honors*—Harry Elijah Belcher, *New York*, Robert Smith Birch, *Pennsylvania* Frederic Leopold Johnson, *New Jersey*, Clifford Abbott Morton, *New Jersey*

ENGLISH. *Honors*—William Miller Gamble, *Pennsylvania*

MATHEMATICS *High Honors* — Howard Herr Yocum, *Pennsylvania*

PHYSICAL SCIENCE. *High Honors*—Philip Ely Robinson, *Pennsylvania*

NATURAL SCIENCE *High Honors* — Richard Frederic Lot Ridgway, *New Jersey*.

SCHOOL OF SCIENCE

Bachelor of Science Course

Milton Floyd Loofbourrow, *Ohio*,	Honorary Oration

[1] School of Science honormen not announced

FELLOWS[1]

Fellow in Classical Literature

Frederic Leopold Johnson,   *New Jersey*

J. S. K. Fellow in Mathematics

Howard Herr Yocum,   *Pennsylvania*

Chancellor Green Fellow in Mental Science

William Emerson Nicely,   *Indiana*

Class of 1860 Fellow in Experimental Science

Philip Ely Robinson,   *Pennsylvania*

Class of 1877 University Fellow in Biology

Chujiro Kochi,[2]   *Japan*

South East Club University Fellow in Social Science

Robert Comin, '97,   *Ohio*

Thaw Fellow in Astronomy

Henry Norris Russell, '97,   *New York*

Special Fellow in Biology

Joseph Edward Kirkwood,[3]   *Oregon*

Special Fellow in Ethics

John Henry Keener, '97,   *Pennsylvania*

PRIZEMEN

Class of 1859 Prize in English Literature

Harry Budd Van Dusen,   *New Jersey*

George Potts Bible Prizes

Roy Paul Miller Davis,   *Michigan*
Harold Bertrand Wells,   *New Jersey*

---

[1] No award of the Boudinot Fellowships in Modern Languages and in History, of the E. M. Biological Fellowship, or of the University Fellowship in Archæology

[2] B. S., Ohio Wesleyan University   [3] B. A., Pacific University

Atwater Prize in Political Science

Harry Budd Van Dusen,   *New Jersey*

Theodore Cuyler Prize in Economics

Clarence Porter Cowles,   *Vermont*

Class of 1869 Prize in Ethics

Charles Harrison Hale,   *Mississippi*

New York Herald Prize

Robert Livingston Beecher,   *British Columbia*

Class of 1876 Prize for Debate in Political Science

Daniel Fickes Altland,   *Pennsylvania*

LYNDE PRIZE DEBATE

Cliosophic Society

Robert Dunning Dripps,   *Pennsylvania*
Matthew Lowrie,   *Pennsylvania*
Robert Livingston Beecher,   *British Columbia*

American Whig Society

Ivy Ledbetter Lee,   *Missouri*
William Frank McCombs,   *Arkansas*
Howard Herr Yocum,   *Pennsylvania*

Lynde Debate Prizemen

Ivy Ledbetter Lee,   First Prize
Matthew Lowrie,   Second Prize
Robert Livingston Beecher,   Third Prize

BAIRD PRIZEMEN

Paul Curtis Martin, *Ohio*,   Baird Prize
William Miller Gamble, *Pennsylvania*,   Oratory
Lester Peck Bryant, *Illinois*,   Delivery
William Miller Gamble, *Pennsylvania*,   Poetry
Howard Herr Yocum, *Pennsylvania*, *First*,   Disputation
Matthew Lowrie, *Pennsylvania*, *Second*,

Junior Honors

Warren Nelson Nevius, *New Jersey*,	
William Magill Schultz, *Pennsylvania*,	First Honor

Junior Orators

Cliosophic Society

Wilson Thomas Moore Beale,	*Pennsylvania*
Conover English,	*New Jersey*
James Henry Harrison,	*New Jersey*
Edward Thompson Newton,	*India*

American Whig Society

Walter Collins Erdman,	*Pennsylvania*
Nathaniel Smith Reeves,	*New York*
Alfred Sewall Weston,	*Maine*
Jay Ralph Woodcock,	*Pennsylvania*

Junior Orator Medalists

Conover English,	First Medal
Walter Collins Erdman,	Second Medal
James Henry Harrison,	Third Medal
Wilson Thomas Moore Beale,	Fourth Medal

Prizemen

Maclean Prize

Walter Collins Erdman,	*Pennsylvania*

Dickinson Prize

Oliver Dimon Kellogg,	*New Jersey*

Thomas B Wanamaker English Prize

Richard Webster,	*New York*

Class of 1870 English Prizes

Richard Webster, *New York*,	Anglo-Saxon
Alexander Armstrong, Jr., *Maryland*,	English Literature [1]

[1] With honorable mention of George Wadsworth Gordon of Illinois

Special Prize in English Philology
De Witt Clinton Croissant,   *District of Columbia*

Stinnecke Scholar
Richard Webster,   *New York*

Sophomore Honors
Class of 1861 Prize[1]
Thomas Jaeger Snyder,   *Pennsylvania*

Francis Biddle Prize[2]
David Laurance Chambers,   *District of Columbia*

Class of 1870 English Prize
David Laurance Chambers,   *District of Columbia*

Freshman Honors
Arthur Herman Adams, *Pennsylvania*,   First Honor

ENTRANCE EXAMINATION PRIZES
Alumni Prize in New York City
Walter Ewing Hope,   *New York*

In Pittsburg
Robert Blakeney Petty, Jr.,   *Pennsylvania*

In Missouri
Carr Lane Glasgow,   *Missouri*

[1] Honorable mention of James Hugh Fleming Moffatt of Maryland
[2] Honorable mention of William Carleton McKee of Pennsylvania

1899

Senior Honors

FIRST GROUP   *Magna cum laude*

Alexander Armstrong, Jr , *Maryland,*   Valedictory Oration
Charles Henry Breed,   *Pennsylvania*
Norman McLeod Carter,   *New York*
Frank Rumsey Elliott,   *Illinois*
George Wadsworth Gordon,   *Illinois*
Oliver Dimon Kellogg,   *New Jersey*
Maxwell Hillegass Kratz,   *Pennsylvania*
Warren Nelson Nevius,   *New Jersey*
William Magill Schultz, *Pennsylvania,*   Latin Salutatory
Alfred Sewall Weston,   *Maine*

Special Honors

PHILOSOPHY   *High Honors* — Maxwell Hillegass Kratz, *Pennsylvania,* Nathaniel Smith Reeves, *New York,* William Magill Schultz, *Pennsylvania*

CLASSICS   *High Honors*—Maxwell Hillegass Kratz *Pennsylvania,* Garrett Stephen Voorhees, *New Jersey,* Richard Webster, *New York*

PHYSICAL SCIENCE.   *High Honors*—Warren Nelson Nevius, *New Jersey.*

HISTORY, JURISPRUDENCE AND POLITICS.   *High Honors*—Alexander Armstrong, Jr , *Maryland,* Alfred Sewall Weston, *Maine*

MATHEMATICS   *High Honors* — Charles Henry Breed, *Pennsylvania,* Oliver Dimon Kellogg, *New Jersey.*   *Honors*—George Heyser Light, *West Virginia*

SCHOOL OF SCIENCE

Bachelor of Science Course   *High Honors*

Edward Charles McWilliams,   *New Jersey*

Honors

Frank Parker Ekings,	*New Jersey*
Robert Potter Elmer,	*New Jersey*
Henry Askew Jackson,	*Delaware*
Mark Moody,	*Missouri*

Civil Engineering Course *High Honors*

John Andrews Ely, Jr , *New York,*   Honorary Oration
Howard Logan,   *Illinois*

Honors

William Henry Detrich,	*Pennsylvania*
Herbert Norris Twells,	*New Jersey*

Fellows[1]

Fellow in Classical Literature

Richard Webster,   *New York*

J S K Fellow in Mathematics

Oliver Dimon Kellogg,   *New Jersey*

Chancellor Green Fellow in Mental Science

Maxwell Hillegass Kratz,   *Pennsylvania*

Class of 1860 Fellow in Experimental Science

Warren Nelson Nevius,   *New Jersey*

Boudinot Fellow in Modern Languages

George Wadsworth Gordon,   *Illinois*

Boudinot Fellow in History

Alfred Sewall Weston,   *Maine*

Class of 1877 University Fellow in Biology

Leonard Worcester Williams,[2]   *Indian Territory*

---

[1] No award of the E M Biological Fellowship or of the University Fellowship in Archæology

[2] B A , Hanover College

South East Club University Fellow in Social Science
John Corliss Dunning,[1]   *Louisiana*

Thaw Fellow in Astronomy
Henry Norris Russell, '97,   *New York*

Charles Scribner University Fellow in English
Hardin Craig,[2]   *Kentucky*

Special Fellow in History
Alexander Armstrong, Jr ,   *Maryland*

Special Fellow in Philosophy
Edward Demoss Miller, '86,   *West Virginia*

Special Fellow in Ethics
Joseph William Lester Jones, '94,   *New Jersey*

Prizemen

Class of 1859 Prize in English Literature
De Witt Clinton Croissant,   *District of Columbia*

George Potts Bible Prizes
Edwin Ernest Curtis, *Pennsylvania,*   First
Alexander Armstrong, Jr , *Maryland,*   Second

Alexander Guthrie McCosh Prize
William Magill Schultz,   *Pennsylvania*

Atwater Prize in Political Science
Herbert Francis Mitchell,   *New Jersey*

Theodore Cuyler Prize in Economics
David Camp Rogers,   *Connecticut*

Class of 1869 Prize in Ethics [3]
Oliver Dimon Kellogg,   *New Jersey*

---

[1] Ph B , Cornell   [2] B A , Centre College
[3] With honorable mention of Charles Henry Breed of Pennsylvania.

New York Herald Prize

Conover English,   *New Jersey*

Class of 1876 Prize for Debate in Political Science

Alfred Sewall Weston,   *Maine*

Lynde Prize Debate

Cliosophic Society

John Hartford Chidester,   *New York*
Conover English,   *New Jersey*
James Henry Northrup,   *New Jersey*

American Whig Society

Herbert Francis Mitchell,   *New Jersey*
Nathaniel Smith Reeves,   *New York*
Alfred Sewall Weston,   *Maine*

Lynde Debate Prizemen

James Henry Northrup,   First Prize
Conover English,   Second Prize
Alfred Sewall Weston,   Third Prize

Baird Prizemen

George Wadsworth Gordon, *Illinois*,   Baird Prize
Walter Collins Erdman, *Pennsylvania*,   Oratory
Conover English, *New Jersey*,   Delivery
Charles Hay Morton, *Kentucky*,   Poetry
Alfred Sewall Weston, *Maine, First*,
Nathaniel Smith Reeves, *New York, Second*,   Disputation

Junior Honors

David Laurance Chambers, *District of Columbia*,
James Hugh Fleming Moffatt, *Maryland*,   First Honor

Junior Orators
Cliosophic Society

David Laurance Chambers,	*District of Columbia*
Herbert Kingsbury England,	*New Jersey*
Charles Miller,	*New Jersey*
William Van Buskirk,	*New York*

American Whig Society

Henry Kilbourne List Dalzell,	*West Virginia*
Joseph Hall Hill,	*Pennsylvania*
James Hugh Fleming Moffatt,	*Maryland*
Charles Kern Smith,	*Pennsylvania*

Junior Orator Medalists

Charles Kern Smith,	First Medal
Charles Miller,	Second Medal
William Van Buskirk,	Third Medal
Herbert Kingsbury England,	Fourth Medal

Prizemen
Maclean Prize

David Laurance Chambers,	*District of Columbia*

Dickinson Prize[1]

Harry Steele Zimmerman,	*Pennsylvania*

Thomas B Wanamaker English Prize

Henry Peter Sanders,	*Maryland*

Class of 1870 English Prizes

Byron Keyser Hunsberger, *Pennsylvania*,	Anglo-Saxon
David Laurance Chambers, *District of Columbia*,	
	English Literature

[1] With honorable mention of Charles Kern Smith of Pennsylvania

Junior German Prizes

Thomas Jaeger Snyder, *Pennsylvania*,	First
Samuel Bryan Scott, *Pennsylvania*,	Second[1]

Sophomore Honors

Class of 1861 Prize

William Lincoln Breckenridge,   *New York*

Francis Biddle Prize[2]

Arthur Herman Adams,   *Pennsylvania*

Class of 1870 English Prize

Walter Ewing Hope,   *New York*

Freshman Honors

Edwin Henry Kellogg, *Pennsylvania*,   First Honor

ENTRANCE EXAMINATION PRIZES

Alumni Prize in New York City

Jasper Hewlett Dodd,	*New Jersey*
Frederick Raymond Whitman,	*New York*

In Philadelphia

Erle Mendenhall Meredith,   *Pennsylvania*

In Pittsburg

Charles Campbell,   *Pennsylvania*

In Central Pennsylvania

Harry Frank Stambaugh,   *Pennsylvania*

---

[1] Honorable mention of Jacob Fischel of New Jersey
[2] Honorable mention of Latta Griswold of New Jersey

1900

Senior Honors

Firsi Group   Magna cum laude

Herbert Douglas Austin,	*Pennsylvania*
Harry John Brandt,	*Missouri*
David Laurance Chambers, *District of Columbia*,	
	Latin Salutatory
Carl Hopkins Elmore,	*Tennessee*
Vernon Lester Hague,	*Iowa*
Adam Miller Hiltebeitel,	*Pennsylvania*
Byron Keyser Hunsberger,	*Pennsylvania*
James Hugh Fleming Moffatt, *Maryland*,	Valedictory Oration
Thomas Jaeger Snyder,	*Pennsylvania*
Leh Roy Urban,	*New Jersey*

Special Honors

PHILOSOPHY.   *High Honors*—William Harper Davis, *Pennsylvania,* Christopher Easton, *New Jersey,* James Hugh Fleming Moffatt, *Maryland,* Samuel Bryan Scott, *Pennsylvania,* Charles Kern Smith, *Pennsylvania*

CLASSICS   *High Honors*—Charles Miller, *New Jersey*

PHYSICAL SCIENCE   *High Honors* — Harry John Brandt, *Missouri*

HISTORY, JURISPRUDENCE AND POLITICS.   *High Honors*—Edward Lawrence Katzenbach, *New Jersey,* Albert Southard Wright, *New Jersey.*   *Honors*—Samuel McDowell, *Pennsylvania.*

MATHEMATICS   *High Honors*—Adam Miller Hiltebeitel, *Pennsylvania*

SCHOOL OF SCIENCE

Bachelor of Science Course   Cum laude

Herbert Ziegler Giffen,	*New Jersey*

Civil Engineering Course   Cum laude

Edward Phinney Hulbert,	*Pennsylvania*

FELLOWS[1]

Fellow in Classical Literature

Herbert Douglas Austin,   *Pennsylvania*

J S K Fellows in Mathematics

Adam Miller Hiltebeitel,   *Pennsylvania*
Oliver Dimon Kellogg, '99,   *New Jersey*
James Caddall Morehead,[2]   *Virginia*

Class of 1860 Fellow in Experimental Science

Harry John Brandt,   *Missouri*

Boudinot Fellow in Modern Languages

Howard McBride,   *Indiana*

Boudinot Fellow in History

Edward Lawrence Katzenbach,   *New Jersey*

University Fellow in Archæology

Aymar Embury, Jr ,   *New York*

Class of 1877 University Fellow in Biology

Earl Douglass,[3]   *Minnesota*

South East Club University Fellow in Social Science

Herbert Frederick Fisher,[4]   *Mississippi*

Thaw Fellow in Astronomy

John Merrill Poor,[5]   *Massachusetts*

Charles Scribner University Fellow in English

Hardin Craig,   *Kentucky*

Special Fellow in History and Archæology

Samuel Bryan Scott,   *Pennsylvania*

---

[1] No award of the Chancellor Green Fellowship in Mental Science, or of the E M Biological Fellowship

[2] B A , Roanoke College   [3] B S , Iowa State College.

[4] B A , University of Mississippi   [5] B A , Dartmouth

Charles Scribner Special Fellow in English
David Laurance Chambers,   *District of Columbia*

Special Fellow in Ethics
Joseph William Lester Jones, '94,   *New Jersey*

Prizemen [1]

Class of 1859 Prize in English Literature
Elmer Schultz Gerhard,   *Pennsylvania*

George Potts Bible Prizes
Samuel Robert Brown, *Pennsylvania*,   First
Byron Keyser Hunsberger, *Pennsylvania*,   Second

Alexander Guthrie McCosh Prize
James Hugh Fleming Moffatt,   *Maryland*

Atwater Prize in Political Science
William Van Buskirk,   *New York*

Frederick Barnard White Prize in Architecture [2]
William Samuel Hammond, Jr.,   *Pennsylvania*

Theodore Cuyler Prize in Economics [3]
Robert Burns Sawyer,   *Illinois*

Class of 1869 Prize in Ethics
Samuel Bryan Scott,   *Pennsylvania*

Lynde Prize Debate

Chosophic Society

William Sanders Elliott,   *Illinois*
Joseph Addison Jones,   *New Jersey*
Samuel McDowell,   *Pennsylvania*

[1] No award of the New York Herald or the C O Joline prizes
[2] With honorable mention of Louis Heffelfinger of Virginia
[3] With honorable mention of Christopher Easton of New Jersey

American Whig Society

Joseph Hall Hill,	*Pennsylvania*
John Bailey Kelly,	*District of Columbia*
Samuel Bryan Scott,	*Pennsylvania*

Lynde Debate Prizemen

Joseph Addison Jones,	First Prize
Joseph Hall Hill,	Second Prize
John Bailey Kelly,	Third Prize

Baird Prizemen[1]

David Lawrance Chambers, *District of Columbia*,	Baird Prize
Charles Miller, *New Jersey*,	Oratory
Herbert Kingsbury England, *New Jersey*,	Delivery
Joseph Addison Jones, *New Jersey, First*,	Disputation
Joseph Hall Hill, *Pennsylvania, Second*,	

Junior Honors

Edward Glassmeyer, *Pennsylvania*,	First Honor

JUNIOR ORATORS

Cliosophic Society

Anstice Ford Eastman,	*New York*
Franklin William Fort,	*New Jersey*
Walter Ewing Hope,	*New York*
Herbert Eugene Shaffer,	*Pennsylvania*

American Whig Society

William Arthur Babson,	*New Jersey*
Howard Edwards Gansworth,	*New York*
George Washington Kehr,	*Pennsylvania*
Ralph Powell Swofford,	*Missouri*

[1] No award of the Baird Prize in Poetry.

Junior Orator Medalists

William Arthur Babson,	First Medal
Anstice Ford Eastman,	Second Medal
Ralph Powell Swofford,	Third Medal
Walter Ewing Hope,	Fourth Medal

PRIZEMEN

Maclean Prize

George Washington Kehr,	*Pennsylvania*

Dickinson Prize

Bert Day Johnson,	*Pennsylvania*

Thomas B Wanamaker English Prize

Edward Glassmeyer,	*Pennsylvania*

Class of 1870 English Prizes

Edward Glassmeyer, *Pennsylvania*,	Anglo-Saxon
Robert Blakeney Petty, Jr., *Pennsylvania*,	English Literature

Junior German Prizes

Edward Glassmeyer, *Pennsylvania*,	First
Charles Enos Snyder Dietz, *Pennsylvania*,	Second

Sophomore Honors

Class of 1861 Prize[1]

Franklin Pierce McDermott, Jr.,	*New Jersey*

Francis Biddle Prize

Harry Frank Stambaugh,	*Pennsylvania*

Class of 1870 English Prize

Edwin Henry Kellogg,	*Pennsylvania*

Stinnecke Scholar

Edwin Henry Kellogg,	*Pennsylvania*

---

[1] With honorable mention of Edwin Henry Kellogg of Pennsylvania

Freshman Honors

Class of 1876 Prize for Debate in Political Science

Axtell Julius Byles,[1]   *Pennsylvania*

ENTRANCE EXAMINATION PRIZES

Alumni Prize in New York City

Corwin Howell,   *New Jersey*

In Chicago

Robert Candee,   *Illinois*

1901

Senior Honors

FIRST GROUP   *Magna cum laude*

William Lincoln Breckenridge,	*New York*
Robert Bartlett Elmore,	*Tennessee*
Edward Glassmeyer, *Pennsylvania*,	Latin Salutatory
Walter Ewing Hope, *New York*,	Valedictory Oration
Howard Rufus Omwake,	*Pennsylvania*
Gordon Macgregor Russell,	*New York*

Special Honors

PHILOSOPHY. *High Honors*—Charles String Gray, *New Jersey,* Merritt Lynde Harding, *Pennsylvania.*

HISTORY, JURISPRUDENCE AND POLITICS. *High Honors*— Clark Silliman Judd, *New York,* Gilbert Walker Kelly, *District of Columbia. Honors*—Walter Ewing Hope, *New York,* Robert Woods Sutton, *Pennsylvania,* Ralph Wentworth, *Massachusetts*

CLASSICS. *High Honors* — Edward Glassmeyer, *Pennsylvania,* Howard Rufus Omwake, *Pennsylvania,* Charles Randal Robbins, *New Jersey,* Beekman Ramsey Terhune, *New Jersey*

---

[1] Of the School of Science

Honors—James Bryce Taylor, *New York,* Howell North White, *New York.*

MATHEMATICS, WITH PHYSICAL SCIENCE.   *High Honors*—William Lincoln Breckenridge, *New York.   Honors* — Harry Gross Dechant, *Pennsylvania*

PHYSICAL SCIENCE.   *High Honors*—Gordon Macgregor Russell, *New York,* Emory J Wilson, *Ohio   Honors*—Bert Day Johnson, *Pennsylvania*

NATURAL SCIENCE.   *High Honors*—Adam Marion Miller, *Pennsylvania.*

SCHOOL OF SCIENCE

Bachelor of Science Course

FIRST GROUP   *Magna cum laude*

George William Marque Maier,	*Iowa*

SECOND GROUP   *Cum laude*

Gordon Taylor Beaham,	*Missouri*
Richard Lawrence Benson,	*Pennsylvania*
Paul Brokaw,	*Missouri*
Wilford Seymour Conrow,	*New York*
Henry Foster Spaulding Frazer,	*New Jersey*
Claude Silbert Hudson,	*Alabama*
P. Clinton Pumyea,	*New Jersey*
George Dickson Richards,	*Illinois*
Thomas Kirkbride Sturdevant,	*Pennsylvania*

Civil Engineering Course

SECOND GROUP   *Cum laude*

John Mifflin Hood, Jr.,	*Maryland*
Louis O'Neill Mellinger,	*Pennsylvania*

FELLOWS[1]

Fellow in Classical Literature

John Kirkwood Mackie,	*Oregon*

[1] No award of the E M Biological Fellowship

J S K Fellows in Mathematics

Oliver Dimon Kellogg, '99,	*New Jersey*
James Caddall Morehead,	*Virginia*
Adam Miller Hiltebeitel, '00,	*Pennsylvania*

Chancellor Green Fellow in Mental Science

Merritt Lynde Harding,	*Pennsylvania*

Class of 1860 Fellow in Experimental Science[1]

Claude Silbert Hudson,	*Alabama*

Boudinot Fellow in Modern Languages

Howard Rufus Omwake,	*Pennsylvania*

Boudinot Fellow in History

Clark Silliman Judd,	*New York*

University Fellow in Archæology

Lee Byrne,	*Illinois*

Class of 1877 University Fellow in Biology

Earl Douglass,[2]	*Minnesota*

South East Club University Fellow in Social Science

Edward Lawrence Katzenbach, '00,	*New Jersey*

Thaw Fellow in Astronomy

John Merrill Poor,	*Massachusetts*

Charles Scribner University Fellow in English

Elmer Schultz Gerhard, '00,	*Pennsylvania*

Special Fellow in History

Henry Jessup Cochran, '00,	*New York*

Special Fellow in Biology

Adam Marion Miller,	*Pennsylvania*

---

[1] With honorable mention of Bert Day Johnson of Pennsylvania

[2] B S , Iowa State College

Special Fellow in History and Archæology
Latta Griswold,   *New Jersey*

Special Fellow in Latin
Howell North White,   *New York*

PRIZEMEN [1]

Class of 1859 Prize in English Literature
Abram Glenni Bartholomew,   *New York*

George Potts Bible Prizes
Henry Meeker Reeve, *New Jersey*,   First
Louis Emery Katzenbach, *New York*,   Second

Alexander Guthrie McCosh Prize
Charles String Gray,   *New Jersey*

Frederick Barnard White Prize in Architecture [2]
Wilford Seymour Conrow,   *New York*

Theodore Cuyler Prize in Economics
Bert Day Johnson,   *Pennsylvania*

Class of 1869 Prize in Ethics
Merritt Lynde Harding,   *Pennsylvania*

New York Herald Prize
Walter Ewing Hope,   *New York*

Class of 1876 Prize for Debate in Political Science
Robert Service Steen,   *Pennsylvania*

LYNDE PRIZE DEBATE
Cliosophic Society
Franklin William Fort,   *New Jersey*
Walter Ewing Hope,   *New York*
Thomas Longland Thompson,   *Michigan*

---

[1] No award of the Atwater or C O Joline prizes
[2] With honorable mention of Jack Randall Crawford of New York

American Whig Society

William Arthur Babson,	*New Jersey*
Robert Service Steen,	*Pennsylvania*
Robert Woods Sutton,	*Pennsylvania*

Lynde Debate Prizemen

William Arthur Babson,	First Prize
Franklin William Fort,	Second Prize
Walter Ewing Hope,	Third Prize

BAIRD PRIZEMEN

Ralph Powell Swofford, *Missouri,*	Baird Prize
William Arthur Babson, *New Jersey,*	Oratory
Walter Ewing Hope, *New York,*	Delivery
Ralph Somerville Thompson, *New York,*	Poetry
Robert Service Steen, *Pennsylvania, First,*	Disputation
Franklin William Fort, *New Jersey, Second,*	

Junior Honors

Harry Frank Stambaugh, *Pennsylvania,*	First Honor

JUNIOR ORATORS

Cliosophic Society

Walter Ewing Evans,	*Pennsylvania*
Edgar Hare Johnson,	*Indiana*
Russell Theodore Mount,	*New Jersey*
Raymond Townley Parrott,	*New Jersey*

American Whig Society

Bond Houser,	*Ohio*
Edwin Henry Kellogg,	*Pennsylvania*
William Teall MacIntyre,	*New York*
Stephen van Rensselaer Trowbridge,	*Turkey*

Junior Orator Medalists

Bond Houser,   First Medal
Russell Theodore Mount,   Second Medal
Edwin Henry Kellogg,   Third Medal
Raymond Townley Parrott,   Fourth Medal

PRIZEMEN

Maclean Prize

Bond Houser,   *Ohio*

Dickinson Prize

Harry Frank Stambaugh,   *Pennsylvania*

Thomas B Wanamaker English Prize [1]

Charles Frederic Reed,   *Pennsylvania*

Class of 1870 English Prizes

Frederick Raymond Whitman, *New York*,   Anglo-Saxon [2]
Edwin Henry Kellogg, *Pennsylvania*,   English Literature [3]

Junior German Prizes

Edward Nelson Teall, *New Jersey*,   First
Arthur Julian Pilgram, *Pennsylvania*,   Second

Stinnecke Scholar

Edwin Henry Kellogg,   *Pennsylvania*

Sophomore Honors

Class of 1861 Prize

Henry Goddard Leach,   *Massachusetts*

Francis Biddle Prize [4]

William Porter Hamilton,   *New Jersey*

---

[1] With honorable mention of Edward Nelson Teall of New Jersey

[2] Honorable mention of Charles Frederic Reed of Pennsylvania, and Arthur Julian Pilgram of Pennsylvania

[3] Honorable mention of Frederick Raymond Whitman of New York.

[4] Honorable mention of George Hamilton Beal of Iowa

Class of 1870 English Prize

Paxton Pattison Hibben,   *Indiana*
Charles Conrad Hewitt,   *New Jersey*

Freshman Honors

ENTRANCE EXAMINATION PRIZES

Alumni Prize in New York City

William Augustus Clark,   *New York*

In Erie

William Elmer Hirt,   *Pennsylvania*

In Northeast Pennsylvania

Daniel Jackson Steward Day,   *Pennsylvania*

ACADEMIC HONORS

1902 [*]

[*] Supplemental.

ACADEMIC HONORS

1902

Senior Honors

FIRST GROUP *Magna cum laude*

Robert Warren Anthony,	*New York*
Bond Houser,	*Ohio*
Edwin Henry Kellogg, *Pennsylvania,*	Valedictory Oration
Ralph John Leibenderfer,	*Ohio*
Russell Theodore Mount,	*New Jersey*
Damon Beckett Pfeiffer,	*New Jersey*
John Edward Semmes, Jr ,	*Maryland*
Herbert Downs Simpson,	*Pennsylvania*
Harry Frank Stambaugh,[1] *Pennsylvania,*	Latin Salutatory
Frederick Raymond Whitman,	*New York*
Raymond Garfield Wright,	*Ohio*

Special Honors

PHILOSOPHY *High Honors*—Edwin Henry Kellogg, *Pennsylvania;* Harry Frank Stambaugh, *Pennsylvania*

HISTORY, JURISPRUDENCE AND POLITICS. *High Honors*—Robert Warren Anthony, *New York,* David Draper Dayton, *Minnesota,* Richard Ely, *New York,* Rex Mackenzie, *Illinois,* Fletcher Swain, *Massachusetts,* Frederick Raymond Whitman, *New York;* Raymond Garfield Wright, *Ohio*

Honors—Louis Herbert Cooke, *New Jersey;* Paul Thornedyke Defrees, *Ohio,* Ralph John Leibenderfer, *Ohio,* Otto Tod Mallery, *Pennsylvania,* Chauncey De Witt Meier, *Ohio,*

---

[1] Stambaugh and Whitman equal for first honor *Minutes of the Faculty,* May 7, 1902

Russell Theodore Mount, *New Jersey,* Arthur Julian Pilgram, *Pennsylvania,* Ernest Cook Poole, *Illinois*

ARCHÆOLOGY AND ART   *High Honors* — John Edward Semmes, Jr , *Maryland*

CLASSICS.   *High Honors* — Jasper Hewlett Dodd, *New Jersey;* Percival Chandler Norris, *New Jersey;* Herbert Downs Simpson, *Pennsylvania*

MODERN LANGUAGES.   *High Honors*—Bond Houser, *Ohio.*

MATHEMATICS   *High Honors* — Ray Gould Brush, *New York,* Edwin Henry Kellogg, *Pennsylvania*

PHYSICAL SCIENCE   *High Honors*—Franklin Pierce Mc-Dermott, Jr., *New Jersey*

NATURAL SCIENCE   *High Honors*—Walter Phillips, *Pennsylvania,* George Howard White, Jr., *Maryland*

SCHOOL OF SCIENCE

Bachelor of Science Course

FIRST GROUP   *Magna cum laude*

Alexander Black,	*Pennsylvania*
Joseph Casper, *New Jersey,*	Honorary Oration

SECOND GROUP   *Cum laude*

William Morris Alrich,	*Pennsylvania*
George Gorman Applegate,	*Pennsylvania*
Sydney Gorham Babson,	*New Jersey*
James Malcolm Bonsall,	*New Jersey*
Harry Russell Bunton,	*Pennsylvania*
Henry Austin Hauxhurst,	*Michigan*
Charles Arbuthnot Lambie,	*Pennsylvania*
William Penn Vail,	*New Jersey*
Clarence Asa Whitehouse,	*Pennsylvania*

Civil Engineering Course

SECOND GROUP   *Cum laude*

Edward Dilworth Latta, Jr.,	*North Carolina*
Edwin Cornelius Luther,	*Pennsylvania*
George William Schusler,	*Pennsylvania*

Fellows[1]

Fellow in Classical Literature

Jasper Hewlett Dodd,   *New Jersey*

J S K Fellows in Mathematics

James Caddall Morehead.   *Virginia*
Archer Everett Young,[2]   *Connecticut*

Chancellor Green Fellow in Mental Science

Harry Frank Stambaugh,   *Pennsylvania*

Class of 1860 Fellow in Experimental Science

Franklin Pierce McDermott, Jr.,   *New Jersey*

Boudinot Fellow in History

Frederick Raymond Whitman,   *New York*

Class of 1877 University Fellow in Biology

Adam Marion Miller, '01,   *Pennsylvania*

South East Club University Fellow in Social Science

Edward Lawrence Katzenbach, '00,   *New Jersey*

Thaw Fellow in Astronomy

Robinson Pierce, Jr ,[3]   *Rhode Island*

Charles Scribner University Fellow in English

De Witt Clinton Croissant '99,   *District of Columbia*

University Fellow in Archæology

Charles Merrill Merwin,   *District of Columbia*

Francis Hinton Maule Fellow in Biology

Walter Phillips,   *Pennsylvania*

---

[1] Boudinot Fellowship in Modern Languages and the E M Biological Fellowship not awarded

[2] B A , Wesleyan University   [3] B A , Brown University

PRIZEMEN [1]

Class of 1859 Prize in English Literature

Robert Haven Schauffler,   *Ohio*

George Potts Bible Prize

Charles Frederic Reed,   *Pennsylvania*

Alexander Guthrie McCosh Prize

Edwin Henry Kellogg,   *Pennsylvania*

Atwater Prize in Political Science

Clarence Valentine Boyer,   *Pennsylvania*

Theodore Cuyler Prize in Economics [2]

Harry Frank Stambaugh,   *Pennsylvania*

Class of 1869 Prize in Ethics

Harry Frank Stambaugh,   *Pennsylvania*

Class of 1876 Prize for Debate in Political Science

Richard Ely,   *New York*

New York Herald Prize

Charles Frederic Reed,   *Pennsylvania*

Frederick Barnard White Prize in Architecture

Charles Merrill Merwin,   *District of Columbia*

LYNDE PRIZE DEBATE

Cliosophic Society

Robert Warren Anthony,   *New York*
Alexander Johnston Barron,   *Pennsylvania*
Richard Ely,   *New York*

American Whig Society

Paul Irvine McElroy,   *Kentucky*
John Green Sims, Jr ,   *Tennessee*
Harry Frank Stambaugh,   *Pennsylvania*

---

[1] Joline Prize in American Political History not awarded
[2] With honorable mention of David Draper Dayton of Minnesota

Lynde Debate Prizemen

Richard Ely,	First Prize
Alexander Johnston Barron,	Second Prize
Robert Warren Anthony,	Third Prize

BAIRD PRIZEMEN

Russell Theodore Mount, *New Jersey*,	Baird Prize
Edwin Henry Kellogg, *Pennsylvania*,	Oratory
Bond Houser,	*Ohio*
John Van Antwerp MacMurray, *New York*,	Poetry
Edwin Henry Kellogg, *Pennsylvania, First*,	
Richard Ely, *New York, Second*,	Disputation

Junior Honors

Frank Smith, *Pennsylvania*,	First Honor[1]

JUNIOR ORATORS
Cliosophic Society

Axtell Julius Byles,	*Pennsylvania*
Corwin Howell,	*New Jersey*
Frank Hoyt Little,	*New Jersey*
Robert B Reed,	*Pennsylvania*

American Whig Society

James Day Brownlee, Jr.,	*Pennsylvania*
Robert Candee,	*Illinois*
Herbert Webb Hopkins,	*New Jersey*
Henry Goddard Leach,	*Massachusetts*

Junior Orator Medalists

Axtell Julius Byles,	First Medal
Robert B Reed,	Second Medal
Corwin Howell,	Third Medal
Robert Candee,	Fourth Medal

---

[1] With honorable mention of Benjamin Edmund Messler of New Jersey

PRIZEMEN

Maclean Prize

Robert Candee,   *Illinois*

Dickinson Prize

John Henry Hankinson,   *New York*

Thomas B Wanamaker English Prize[1]

Walter Franklin Hollenbach,   *Pennsylvania*

Class of 1870 English Prizes

Frank Smith, *Pennsylvania*,   Anglo-Saxon[2]
Harry Christian Schweikert, *Pennsylvania*, English Literature[3]

Junior German Prizes

Paxton Pattison Hibben, *Indiana*,   First
Gilbert Fairchild Close, *Pennsylvania*,   Second

Sophomore Honors[4]

Class of 1861 Prize

Dwight Woodbridge Edwards,   *Minnesota*

Class of 1870 English Prize

Louis Banigan, *New Jersey*,
Phillips Alexander Moore, *Pennsylvania*,   Equal

Freshman Honors[5]

ENTRANCE EXAMINATION PRIZES

Alumni Prize in New York City

Charles Christopher Mierow,   *New Jersey*

---

[1] Frank Smith, Pennsylvania, honorable mention

[2] Harry Christian Schweikert, Pennsylvania, honorable mention

[3] Charles Conrad Hewitt, New Jersey, honorable mention

[4] Francis Biddle Prize not awarded

[5] First Honor Prize discontinued

APPENDIX

UNIVERSITY DEBATERS

1892–'93

First Yale-Princeton debate held at Princeton, March 15, 1893   Question: "*Resolved*, That the peaceful annexation of Canada would be beneficial to the United States."

Princeton   Affirmative

Jay Falconer Ewing, '93,	*Iowa*
Donald MacColl, '94,	*New York*
Benjamin William M'Cready Sykes, '94,	*New Jersey*

No decision

1893–'94 [1]

1894–'95

Second Yale-Princeton debate held at New Haven, May 1, 1895.   Question· "*Resolved*, That the Income Tax Law of 1894 was, under the circumstances, a justifiable one."

Princeton   Affirmative

William Foster Burns, '95,	*Illinois*
Benjamin Lewis Hirshfield, '95,	*Ohio*
Robert McNutt McElroy, '96,	*Missouri*

Won by Princeton

First Harvard-Princeton debate held at Princeton, March 27, 1895   Question· "*Resolved*, That if it were possible, a

---

[1] No debate with Yale.

reasonable property qualification for the exercise of municipal franchise in the United States would be desirable "

Princeton   Affirmative

Willis Howard Butler, '95,	*New York*
Joseph William Park, '95,	*Mississippi*
Howard Erskine White, '95,	*New York*

Won by Harvard

1895–'96

Third Yale-Princeton debate held at Princeton, December 6, 1895   Question. "*Resolved*, That it would be wise to establish, in respect to all State legislation of a general character, a system of referendum similar to that established in Switzerland."

Princeton   Affirmative

Edward William Hamilton, '96,	*New York*
Ralph Barton Perry, '96,	*New York*
Robert Ogilvie Kirkwood, 97,	*New York*

Won by Yale

Second Harvard-Princeton debate held at Cambridge, March 13, 1896   Question. "*Resolved*, That Congress should take immediate steps toward the complete retirement of all legal tender notes "

Princeton   Affirmative

Frederick William Loetscher, '96,	*Iowa*
Robert McNutt McElroy, '96,	*Missouri*
Herbert Ure, '96,	*New Jersey*

Won by Harvard

1896–'97

Third Harvard-Princeton debate held at Princeton, December 18, 1896 Question. "*Resolved*, That, assuming the adoption of adequate constitutional amendments, the United States should adopt a system of responsible cabinet government."

Princeton   Affirmative

Robert McNutt McElroy, '96,	*Missouri*
Robert Fulton Sterling, '97,	*Pennsylvania*
Howard Herr Yocum, '98,	*Pennsylvania*

Won by Harvard

Fourth Yale-Princeton debate held at New Haven, May 7, 1897. Question. "*Resolved*, That the power of the Speaker of the House of Representatives is detrimental to the public interests."

Princeton   Negative

Robert Fulton Sterling, '97,	*Pennsylvania*
Howard Herr Yocum, '98,	*Pennsylvania*
Nathaniel Smith Reeves, '99,	*New York*

Won by Princeton

1897–'98

Fifth Yale-Princeton debate held at Princeton, March 25, 1898. Question. "*Resolved*, That national party lines should be disregarded in the choice of councils and administrative officials in the United States."

Princeton   Negative

Matthew Lowrie, '98,	*Pennsylvania*
Howard Herr Yocum, '98,	*Pennsylvania*
William Magill Schultz, '99,	*Pennsylvania*

Won by Yale

Fourth Harvard-Princeton debate held at Cambridge, May
11, 1898   Question "*Resolved*, That the present restrictions
on immigration into the United States are insufficient "

Princeton   Negative

Robert Dunning Dripps, '98,	*Pennsylvania*
Matthew Lowrie, '98,	*Pennsylvania*
Nathaniel Smith Reeves, '99,	*New York*

Won by Harvard

1898 –'99

Sixth Yale-Princeton debate held at New Haven, December 6, 1898. Question "*Resolved*, That the United States
should annex Cuba "

Princeton   Affirmative

Conover English, '99,	*New Jersey*
Nathaniel Smith Reeves, '99,	*New York*
Joseph Addison Jones, '00,	*New Jersey*

Won by Yale

Fifth Harvard-Princeton debate held at Princeton, April
5, 1899   Question "*Resolved*, That a formal alliance between
the United States and Great Britain for the protection and
advancement of their common interests is advisable."

Princeton   Affirmative

James Henry Northrup, '99,	*New Jersey*
Nathaniel Smith Reeves, '99,	*New York*
Alfred Sewall Weston, '99,	*Maine*

Won by Harvard

1899 –'00

Sixth Harvard-Princeton debate held at Cambridge, December 15, 1899   Question "*Resolved*, That the English
claims in the controversy with the South African Republic are
justifiable "

Princeton *Negative*

Alfred Sewall Weston, '99,   *Maine*
Joseph Hall Hill, '00,   *Pennsylvania*
Joseph Addison Jones, '00,   *New Jersey*

Won by Harvard

Seventh Yale-Princeton debate held at Princeton, May 8, 1900   Question. "*Resolved*, That the Hay-Pauncefote Treaty should be ratified in the form in which it was originally submitted to the Senate (it being understood that any change in the terms of the treaty or any action by the Senate affecting the treaty is not germane to the question at issue)."

Princeton *Negative*

Joseph Hall Hill, '00,   *Pennsylvania*
Joseph Addison Jones, '00,   *New Jersey*
Robert Service Steen, '01,   *Pennsylvania*

Won by Princeton

1900–'01

Eighth Yale-Princeton debate held at New Haven, March 27, 1901   Question. "*Resolved*, That a system of subsidies, other than the present mail subsidies, should be adopted by the United States to encourage our shipbuilding and ocean-carrying trades "

Princeton *Negative*

Walter Ewing Hope, '01,   *New York*
Robert Service Steen, '01,   *Pennsylvania*
Axtell Julius Byles, '03,   *Pennsylvania*

Won by Princeton

Seventh Harvard-Princeton debate held at Princeton, May 10, 1901. Question. "*Resolved*, That Congress was justified in imposing the terms embodied in the Platt Amendment to the Army Appropriation Bill, as conditions precedent to

leaving the government and control of Cuba to its people (the
condition with regard to the Isle of Pines being excepted)."

Princeton   Affirmative

William Arthur Babson, '01,	*New Jersey*
Walter Ewing Hope, '01,	*New York*
Robert Service Steen, '01,	*Pennsylvania*

Won by Harvard

1901 –'02

Ninth Yale-Princeton debate held at Princeton, December 6, 1901   Question· "*Resolved*, That the adoption of the
Fifteenth Amendment to the Constitution of the United States
has been justified."

Princeton   Affirmative

Robert Warren Anthony, '02,	*New York*
James Jackson Forstall, '03,	*Illinois*
John Ewing Steen, '03,	*Pennsylvania*

Won by Yale

Eighth Harvard-Princeton debate held at Cambridge,
March 26, 1902.   Question   "*Resolved*, That Mayor Low
should strictly enforce the excise law in New York City "

Princeton   Affirmative

Robert Warren Anthony, '02,	*New York*
Alexander Johnston Barron, '02,	*Pennsylvania*
Robert Andrew Blair, P G ,	*Ireland*

Won by Princeton

INDEX

INDEX

Italics refer to notes

www.ingramcontent.com/pod-product-compliance
Lightning Source LLC
LaVergne TN
LVHW011352180726
843640LV00005B/1238